Build Your Own Mutual Fund

How to Use a Personal Portfolio to Take Control of Your Financial Life

Brian O'Connell

Adams Media
Avon, Massachusetts

My deepest gratitude to my patient wife and three beautiful children who tolerated my presence during the writing of this book. Special thanks to my agent, Stacey Glick, who provided a steady hand from day one. Also, a tip of the cap to Jill Alexander, my editor at Adams Media, who maintained her composure and good humor when the author was forever testing her patience. She aced that test.

Published by
Adams Media, an F+W Publications Company
57 Littlefield Street, Avon, MA 02322. U.S.A.
www.adamsmedia.com

ISBN: 1-58062-930-X

Printed in The United States of America.

J I H G F E D C B A

Library of Congress Cataloging-in-Publication Data
O'Connell, Brian.
Build your own mutual fund / Brian O'Connell.
p.   cm.
ISBN 1-58062-930-X
1. Portfolio management. 2. Investment analysis. 3. Finance,
Personal. I. Title.
HG4529.5.O32   2004
332.6--dc21   2003012789

This publication is designed to provide accurate and authoritative information with regard to the subject matter covered. It is sold with the understanding that the publisher is not engaged in rendering legal, accounting, or other professional advice. If legal advice or other expert assistance is required, the services of a competent professional person should be sought.
—From a *Declaration of Principles* jointly adopted by a Committee of the American Bar Association and a Committee of Publishers and Associations

Many of the designations used by manufacturers and sellers to distinguish their products are claimed as trademarks. Where those designations appear in this book and Adams Media was aware of a trademark claim, the designations have been printed with initial capital letters.

This book is available at quantity discounts for bulk purchases.
For information, call 1-800-872-5627.

Contents

Introduction

The mutual fund industry has had a great run, hasn't it?

Launched in the 1920s, when a group of Boston financial industry executives pooled their money and started the first mutual fund, the Massachusetts Investors Trust, with $50,000 in assets, the fund industry changed the way Americans invested.

No longer could only the rich and privileged get professional money management. With the mutual fund—common folks could, too.

Over the years, the fund industry has grown into a $7 trillion behemoth, with its vast tentacles snaking through every financial bourse in the world. The 1990s was the heyday of the mutual fund, with double-digit annual returns the norm and investors lining up waving their checkbooks for the chance to deposit their money in a favorite fund.

But, along the way, something happened. Although technology breakthroughs like the Internet enabled investors to become more knowledgeable and gave them more investment options, the fund industry didn't grow along with its customers.

Instead, by the time the early 2000s rolled around, fund shareholders still got the same high fees, high tax bills, and inflexible fund framework that they'd always gotten, only this time without the performance returns they'd grown accustomed to.

Investors looked at their quarterly fund statements, and for the first time they started noticing the high fees and onerous tax liabilities. They suddenly realized that they had no control over the stocks selected in a given fund. Many began looking for a better way.

A New Way to Invest

Enter the "personal portfolio."

Wall Street knows that investors can forego mutual fund firms and put together their own portfolio of twenty to fifty stocks and pay only $200 to $300 a year in brokerage fees for the privilege. Wall Street also knows that it's easy to put together two or three such portfolios and pay no additional charge. It just doesn't want investors to know. Now, with *Build Your Own Mutual Fund*, the secret's finally out.

Personal portfolios are already stealing away billions in business from the venerable, but increasingly archaic, mutual funds. In fact, scores of Wall Street experts predict personal portfolios will snatch $1 trillion in assets from mutual funds in the next decade. According to the Washington, D.C.–based Money Management Institute, investors are already pouring around $450 billion into personal portfolios.

Why, in the current economic climate, with oil prices rising and investor confidence in a constant state of flux, are "folios" so popular? Ease of use, more control, lower fees, and a better tax picture—just for starters. With self-created mutual funds, investors get the low-cost diversification and professional stock-picking benefits they get from mutual funds, but in any combination they want.

How Folios Work

How do individual mutual funds work? Simple. They harness the power of the Internet so that individual investors can buy and sell entire stock portfolios with just a few mouse clicks, instead of having to pick individual stocks or mutual funds. With customized funds, investors choose their risk, industry, or other personal investing preferences; they then directly invest in whole portfolios that match those preferences. For a flat fee of about $300 a year, consumers can assemble up to three baskets, or "folios," each containing as many as fifty stocks.

The consumer can select stocks, or they can be handpicked from a long list of specialty prefab portfolios. Once the basket is in hand, investors can trade the stocks it contains, rebalance the folio as often as desired, or trade it in its entirety.

Like mutual funds, folios invest in a portfolio of stocks, instead of just a handful of stocks, thus providing investors with a lower level of risk for the same expected rate of return, or the potential for a higher expected rate of return for the same level of risk. Unlike mutual funds, folios come with additional benefits. Gone are the minimum investment requirements and expense ratio bills. Gone is frustration over lack of input in a fund's selection. Gone is the ethereal sense of detachment from not actually owning the stocks. By combining model portfolios with advice, trade execution, and favorable fee schedules, the personal portfolio firms appeal to many segments of the individual investing community.

What Is This Book About?

Build Your Own Mutual Fund is a blow-by-blow account of why fed-up mutual fund investors are turning to building their own mutual funds with the help of "personal portfolio" investment firms—and a "how to" primer for those investors who want to.

This book walks the average investor through the process of building his or her own mutual fund—safely, cheaply, and with more benefits than he's been receiving from his "professionally managed" mutual funds.

In this book, I'll . . .

* Explain to you why folios are the future of Wall Street. I'll demonstrate why folios and today's newly empowered investors are a perfect match (and why mutual funds aren't).
* Show you the best ways to invest in folios; detail the best asset allocation and risk management investment strategies; demonstrate why folios are the best choice for socially

responsible investors; and lay out the best and brightest online folio firms that are vying for the attention of investors.

- Teach you how to choose a personal investment portfolio; how to choose a personal portfolio manager; how to tackle tax issues; how to use the Internet to find specific separate accounts (such as socially responsible or emerging market-flavored accounts); and much, much more.

After reading *Build Your Own Mutual Fund*, you will walk away with the tools and talent to radically change the way you invest. You'll view investing in a revolutionary new way, and you—along with a burgeoning army of your fellow Americans—will become your very own mutual fund manager.

Why Should You Read This Book?

Dissatisfaction among mutual fund investors toward mutual fund companies is just now bubbling to the surface. Three straight years of bad performance coupled with high tax bills have fueled an unprecedented backlash against the fund industry, leading to an aggressive search by investors for an alternative to mutual funds that has all the benefits of the traditional mutual fund but without its high fees, inflexible tax structure, and lack of control.

Standing in the way of further personal portfolio growth is the notion that investors aren't qualified to build their own mutual funds and that they will take on too much risk in trying to do so. It's an attitude being fostered by the fund companies that don't want to give up a single nickel of the $7 trillion mutual fund market.

## Chapter 1

The Death of Mutual Funds?

"Money is indeed the most important thing in the world; and all sound and successful personal and national morality should have this fact for its basis."

—George Bernard Shaw

The date was April 25, 2002. The venue was the Financial Planning Association's "Forum 2002" conference in New York City. The speaker was Vanguard Group founder John Bogle. The agenda? The demise of mutual funds.

Bogle, an often-controversial public speaker known for taking his mutual fund brethren to task, looked out over the jampacked ballroom and told advisors the last thing they wanted to hear. Mutual funds, he said, were in trouble. Big trouble.

He read a laundry list of complaints that investors had recently begun harboring toward mutual funds. Fees were way too high. Funds were horribly tax-inefficient. Mutual funds were inflexible and changed managers too much. There were too many of them, with roughly 120 technology funds alone added in the last few years of the dot-com bubble. Above all, Bogle told the audience, mutual fund companies didn't have their investors' best interests at heart anymore. In a $7 trillion mutual fund marketplace, the game had changed from accommodating shareholder concerns to steamrolling them in the name of grabbing more market share.

It was no accident that the title of Bogle's speech was "The End of Mutual Fund Dominance." For years, Wall Street experts had whispered that the death of mutual funds was near. Their fear was that a patchwork quilt of alternative investment tools under the individually managed portfolio banner—tools that gave investors more control over their portfolios for a lot less money—would take the place of mutual funds in the hearts and minds of American investors. Such tools included separate accounts, managed accounts, wrap accounts, and personal investment portfolios. All emphasized investor control for a reasonable cost. All emphasized a "take control" approach. All have gained on mutual funds in recent years, lending some credence to the cacophony of voices that have predicted the downfall of mutual funds.

One well-respected business consulting group—Forrester Research—went so far as to publish a report in October 2001 entitled "The End of Mutual Fund Dominance." In it, Forrester, says that the rate of mutual fund growth is slowing just as the rate of personal portfolio plans is rising. The study projected that mutual fund assets will grow by 26 percent and separate account assets will grow by 400 percent by 2004, a year that should (according to Forrester) signal the fund industry's demise. Another firm, Boston's Financial Research Corp., says that privately managed account assets are expected to grow 20 percent a year, to $1 trillion in 2005, having already quadrupled since the mid-1990s.

"For years, mutual funds have been U.S. investors' No. 1 way to invest," said Jaime Punishill, senior analyst at Forrester, in its report. "By offering all the benefits of funds—without the detriments—new approaches to online investing will force more than $1 trillion worth of assets to exit mutual funds." Faced with massive outflows and enormous pressure on fees, Forrester expects the ballooning number of mutual funds to reverse, leaving just 5,000 funds by 2010.

Even so, for the $7 trillion mutual fund industry, a loss of $1 trillion is akin to putting a dent in your Cadillac. It's hardly good news, true. But it won't keep your car off the road—for now. Even if the growth rate of mutual funds slowed from its present rate of roughly 20 percent to 10 percent annually, even that would be enough to put $18 trillion into mutual fund company coffers by 2018.

The Rise of Personal Portfolios

The real danger to the mutual funds industry—and the real opportunity for average investors who like the idea of professional money management but want the low cost and high flexibility that funds are not currently providing—is the highly alluring idea of building your own mutual funds.

Over the years, portfolios have been the investment strategy of choice among wealthy Americans who wanted personal investment advice and who could afford to pay for it. Now, as widespread technology innovation and cutthroat competition among investment firms have brought the price of doing business on Wall Street down, investors of all stripes and income levels can get in on the action. That's exactly what *personal* portfolios do. With the personal portfolio, investors can choose their own "baskets" of mutual funds for as little as $14.95 (the basic rate at online personal portfolio service FOLIO*fn*).

Higher-end help is available, too, in the "separate accounts" market. Separate accounts allow investors with portfolio assets of $50,000 or more—a small amount in this day and age—to build their own mutual fund portfolios, with the help of a money manager and personal financial advisor for about one or two percent of total portfolio assets, a third or more less than they'd pay for a traditional open-ended mutual fund.

The sky is the limit for personal portfolios, especially if 401(k) account plan sponsors slash their traditional ties to mutual funds and turn to personal portfolios in response to heightened consumer demand for such investment vehicles (a highly likely scenario, according to the Forrester report).

Growing Investor Complaints Toward Mutual Funds

Mutual fund shareholders are ticked off. And who can blame them? Fund performance has been down for years while the fees for investing in them keep rising. Here are the primary reasons investors are down on mutual funds:

- The price tag. According to financial writer Mary Rowland, the average expense ratio of a domestic stock fund is more than 1.5 percent, money that is skimmed off your investment dollar every year.
- What's in my fund? Mutual fund firms are obliged to report holdings only twice a year. By the time the statements arrive in shareholders' mailboxes, the news is months old— way too late to make any changes.
- Driving a DeSoto in a Corvette world. Mutual funds post their prices only once a day, a lifetime in an Internet-dominated "real time" culture where many investment Web sites post security prices every 30 seconds.
- Paying Uncle Sam regardless of performance. Mutual funds can be the financial version of root canal surgery, as shareholder tax liabilities are affected by the number of times a fund manager trades stocks in and out of the fund during the year. What does the mutual fund company care? It just hands the capital gains tax bill to shareholders.

The New Kid on the Block

What is there to like about personal portfolios? Plenty, as it turns out. Personal portfolios, also known as "folios" in Wall Street circles, enable average Americans to bypass those high mutual fund fees and awful brokerage commissions and build (and own) their own personal mutual funds. That means choosing the stocks that comprise a fund (usually without the direct help of a financial advisor or money manager, though personal portfolio providers offer help), managing the portfolio, and customizing the portfolio periodically to satisfy one's own objectives.

With the typical personal portfolio, investors can buy anywhere from one to fifty stocks in a given investment category, preselected by the folio provider to meet common investment objectives such as growth, balance, or capital preservation. Normally, as in the case of FOLIO*fn*, the total amount of stocks you can buy is limited to about 3,800 listed securities—roughly 95 percent of the amount of stocks listed on the New York Stock Exchange and NASDAQ. While that number does include the most commonly traded stocks on Wall Street (like IBM, Microsoft, Procter & Gamble, and some of the newer, hotter technology and biotechnology companies), it can cost extra—around $15 per transaction—to buy stocks outside of the 3,500 listed.

Typically, investors can trade in their personal folios twice daily, giving them ample—but not unlimited—opportunity to change the complexity of their personal portfolios. Folio providers make investors' portfolios readily available for easy viewing and updating, almost always in the form of "portfolio tracking" pages on their company Web sites.

Advantages of Personal Portfolios

With personal portfolios, investors can manage their folios any way they like. If, for example, tax liability is a big concern for a given investor, he or she can create built-in "triggers" in their portfolios (again, with the help of the folio company) that automatically sell a security or two to meet tax-planning objectives and to avoid a big year-end tax bill. Try doing *that* with a mutual fund.

Companies that market personal portfolios—such as FOLIO*fn*, E*Trade, Quick & Reilly, and Charles Schwab—say they give investors the diversification advantages of mutual funds, plus more control over fees and taxes, and the added bonus of direct stock ownership.

Point by point, it's hard to argue with personal portfolios. Here's a more detailed look at some of their advantages.

Simplicity and Control

The ability to build their own mutual funds is highly appealing to those post-Enron investors who want more control over their financial lives. Consequently, prepackaged baskets of stocks that average investors can buy and trade for a flat fee—and that enable them to save on fees, keep taxes low, and customize their portfolios—are proving extremely popular.

Why individual portfolios? In two words—simplicity and control. You call the shots, not some fresh-faced twenty-four-year-old Wharton graduate who just moved out of his parents' house for the first time. If, for example, you want to hold onto a long-term winner like Disney or General Electric, you can. Unlike most mutual fund companies, you don't have to sell your winners for tax reasons.

Then there's the simplicity angle. Personal portfolios are much like index mutual funds, which try to match a stock index like the Standard & Poor's 500. It's a low-cost, no-nonsense approach that has spanked the average stock mutual fund for more than a decade. Because index funds do relatively little trading, they generate little in the way of capital gains and therefore appeal to the buy-and-hold investor. It's much the same story for personal portfolios—only with even lower fees and more control.

The "Starter Kit" Advantage

Investors who lack the know-how to create their own mutual funds from scratch can choose from "thematic" funds offered by folio companies. This means that an investor who can't make up her mind about which biotech stocks to buy can go ahead and select an existing biotech portfolio comprised of thirty of the sector's most popular stocks. Sounds like a mutual fund, right? It is, except for the tax benefits, lower fees, and

6

higher trading control of a biotech folio versus a traditional biotechnology mutual fund.

Tax Efficiency

Portfolios are much more tax-efficient than owning a standard mutual fund, as folio owners don't have a remote mutual fund manager selling their appreciated stocks whenever he or she wants to, a situation that can fuel a vicious tax liability for the unwary fund investor. With folios, you can trade off winners against losers to neutralize most of your tax liability. You also avoid the hassle of selling each stock position at a time, since you can execute the batch trades.

One additional factor to take into account: If you hold your traditional fund in a taxable account, you will have to pay taxes on your share of any capital gains and dividend income distributions. With personal portfolios, you incur no capital gains taxes unless you elect to sell some of the stocks within your "basket."

Lower Fees

The annual cost of a personal portfolio—about $300—is significantly less than a garden-variety mutual fund. For example, if you bought a traditional mutual fund instead of a stock basket from BuyandHold.com or FOLIO*fn*, you'd be assessed management fees averaging 1.43 percent annually, according to Morningstar Research. For a $50,000 mutual fund, these fees would be around $700 per year; with larger funds the difference in cost between personal portfolios and mutual funds would be even greater.

Diversity (with a Twist)

Another big difference between personal portfolios and mutual funds is the ability to select the stocks you want within certain investment sectors. For example, FOLIO*fn* enables investors to select from seventy-five prepackaged baskets, which blanket a wide spectrum of asset categories. One folio is made up of ADRs (American Depositary Receipts) of Latin American stocks, for example. Another folio contains stocks of companies with the highest percentage of women investors. Still another folio holds stocks of companies that have absolutely no connection with the manufacture or sale of tobacco products. Other folios more closely resemble exchange-traded index funds since they're composed of stocks in sectors such as technology, telecommunications, and so forth. Investors can also choose folios made up of small-, mid-, and large-cap stocks.

It's an Online World

In an age when information is as much a commodity as widgets or washing machines, the creation and maintenance of personal portfolios is mostly done online via the Internet. That's where investors want to be, as evidenced by a recent study by Forrester that says equity assets managed on the Internet will grow to $1.56 trillion by 2003, from just $246 billion in 1999. It is also estimated that the number of accounts will grow from 5.4 million to 20.4 million over the same period. Investors are lured to the Web by the simplicity and immediacy of online investing. Just by clicking a few keys on a personal computer, personal portfolio owners can buy and sell fully diversified portfolios of hundreds of stocks for a flat monthly or annual fee that could very well be less than your monthly cable or dry cleaning bill.

Anyone Can Play

With personal portfolios, there's no required minimum amount to open an account and no minimum for each trade. (This is not true for separate accounts, a different form of individually managed portfolios; usually, you have to have at least $50,000 to open a separate account.) That makes personal portfolios very appealing to investors who only want to put small amounts into their account each quarter.

More Advantages

In a snapshot, here are some other advantages of personal portfolios:

- No need to play catch up. With a folio, you can assemble a long-term portfolio quickly.
- As a long-term stockholder, you could avoid most capital gains taxes. If you did sell, you could match winners and losers and keep taxes to a bare minimum.
- As a stockholder, you can vote in corporate proxy fights.
- You can benefit from stock splits and spinoffs.
- If you're a socially conscious investor, you can sell stocks you find objectionable, such as alcohol or tobacco companies.

Socially Responsible Investors and Personal Portfolios

Assets in socially screened investment portfolios under professional management rose by more than a third from 1999 to 2001 to top the $2 trillion mark for the first time ever, according to the Social Investment Forum's "Report on Responsible Investing Trends in the United States, November 2001." The 36 percent growth rate is more than 1.5 times the 22 percent rise reported for all investment assets under professional management in the United States during the same two-year period.

The SIF says much of the growth is attributable to the rise in individual investment accounts. That's because personal portfolio investors can pick and choose their own stocks. If an antitobacco investor doesn't want Philip Morris in her mutual fund, tough luck. It's not her call. But a folio investor can cut such companies out in seconds if so desired. And apparently, many do so desire. According to the study, assets in separate accounts managed for institutional clients and individual investors grew by nearly 40 percent from 1999 to

2001. These socially screened private portfolios rose to $1.87 trillion in 2001 from $1.343 billion in 1999, from $433 billion in 1997, and up from just $150 billion in 1995.

Clearly, personal investment portfolios are having an impact on socially responsible investing.

Growth of Personal Portfolios versus Mutual Funds

While personal portfolios may not knock mutual funds off their perch anytime soon, they're sure making progress.

In 2001, the Boston investment analytical firm Cerulli Associates released a study that said the growth in separate accounts has outpaced the growth in mutual funds for the past three and a half years by between 2.5 and 6.7 percentage points annually.

Consequently, Cerulli believes that fund companies may take a "if you can't beat 'em, join 'em," mentality and begin creating their own folio offerings. While that wouldn't be good news for the online folio start-up firms that have hit the marketplace in the last two or three years, imagine a Fidelity Investments or a Vanguard Group competing against a small folio company—it would be great news for investors, who would have more personal portfolio choices than ever. ❖

Nothing's Perfect

Granted, personal portfolios aren't for everybody. If you're a risk-averse investor who is uncomfortable calling the shots, personal folios probably aren't right for you. Chances are a good index mutual fund would allow you to sleep better at night.

Correspondingly, if you itch to become a professional trader and want to pull the trigger and trade ten, twenty, or even thirty times a day, personal portfolios don't allow you to do that. For those risk-takers, a solid discount brokerage firm may offer a better alternative.

But for the average investor who is sick and tired of being kicked around by indifferent mutual fund companies, and who wants to take more control over his or her financial fortunes while paying lower fees and enjoying more tax flexibility, it's hard to argue with personal portfolios.

After all, when John Bogle, the founder of one of the most powerful mutual fund houses in the world, says that the mutual fund industry is in trouble, isn't it time to start looking at alternatives?

What's the Downside?

Due to their nascent status in the investment firmament, personal portfolios are largely untested, performance wise. Thus, it's possible that even with its fee and tax advantages, your overall folio performance may lag the performance of your most recent, similarly constructed mutual fund.

Also, the folio firms that market personal portfolios may begin to find that it is economically unfeasible to track and manage thousands of individual investor portfolios rather than the dozen or so mutual funds that a mid-size fund company has to account for. That said, innovations in online investing circles have been constant in recent years, suggesting that the problem of keeping track of personal portfolios may really be no problem at all.

Case Study: *Tale of a Mutual Fund Dropout*

Danielle Clemmer had the last laugh.

Clemmer, a thirty-something fashion designer with a tiny Greenwich Village loft and a growing business with one of New York's leading design firms, hardly ever paid attention to her mutual fund performance.

But when, after years of growth, the market went into a tailspin in 2000, Danielle began reading her statements more closely. She didn't like what she saw.

"I couldn't believe the fees and add-ons they were getting away with," Danielle says. "I'd never noticed it before, because I was making money and wasn't really paying attention."

Now that times were lean, Danielle began resenting the fact that her fund company kept raking in the fees even though the fund's performance was way down. "I know it sounds naïve, but I wanted them to share some of the pain, too. Fat chance."

Determined to do something, Danielle brought her statement home to her parents' house one Thanksgiving. Her father, a CPA, knew something about numbers and began pointing out how restrictive her funds were when it came to taxes. "He told me that I was paying taxes for the fund even in years when it lost 10 or 20 percent."

Her father also pointed out how Danielle, a strict non-smoker, was investing in tobacco company stocks through her large-cap value fund. "That was the straw that broke the camel's back—no pun intended," she laughs. "I needed to move my money somewhere else where I had more control."

Madison, a friend from work, told her about a new way to invest in "baskets" of stocks that emulated mutual funds, but without the fees, taxes, and loss-of-control issues. "Maddie was dating a guy on Wall Street who had begun investing in folios, which he described as a way to build your own mutual funds but at a reduced cost and with much more flexibility. That sounded great to me."

Danielle immediately contacted the folio firm and opened an account. With her dad's help, she selected about twenty stocks that she liked and that fit her investing goals. "Now my portfolio has bounced back and I only had to pay $29.95 per month for the privilege. And I got rid of the tobacco stocks, too."

Better yet, she cashed out of her mutual fund and used the proceeds to fund her new folio campaign. "Later I heard that my fund firm was going into the folio business," she laughs. "I guess I beat them to it."

Danielle Clemmer Personal Portfolio
ALLOCATION PERCENTAGES
60% stable value stocks
20% conservative equity income stocks
10% Treasury bonds
10% cash
FOLIO FAVORITES
Caterpillar, Inc., Alcoa

Chapter Checklist

High fees, onerous taxes, and loss of control—not to mention loss of performance—are causing investors to take a closer look at their mutual funds.

✓ Even the mutual fund industry's own leaders are speaking openly about the end of fund era dominance.

✓ Forrester Research says that personal portfolios are growing by a much wider margin than mutual funds.

✓ Personal portfolios enable investors to build and customize their own "mutual funds" any way they like.

✓ Personal portfolios are easily affordable for investors of all stripes. Fees, taxes, and having greater control all favor folios over funds.

✓ Are folios for you? If you prefer someone else making your investment decisions—probably not.

Chapter 2

How Folios Work

Holdup Man: "Quit stalling—I said your money or your life!"
Jack Benny: "I'm thinking it over!"

—*THE JACK BENNY PROGRAM*

I t was the philosopher Aristotle who said that the way to achieve success is to first have a clear, definitive goal. Then you have to have the necessary means to achieve that goal—wisdom, money, materials, and methods. Lastly, adjust all your means to that end.

When it comes to building your own mutual fund, your first objective should be: How do I go about it?

It's a big question. Sure, you can go off willy-nilly and begin buying stocks from discount brokers until you have twenty or thirty of them and call that a mutual fund. But is it really a mutual fund?

I don't think so. Without some formal mechanism for building your own fund and gaining all the adherent advantages associated with having your own personal mutual fund—the tax breaks, the lower fees, the increased flexibility—you're really no better off than you would be with the high fees, high taxes, and limited flexibility of an actively managed mutual fund.

Other perceived fund-building options you might be considering include the exchange traded funds or even the index mutual fund (this type of fund tracks a specific asset class index, like the Dow Jones Industrials or the Russell 2000 Small Cap Index, and mirrors them in the fund's holdings).

These may sound like a good idea upon first look. Index funds and exchange traded funds are easy to follow and offer lower fees than traditional mutual funds. The trouble with such investment options is that you don't get to pick the stocks you want in your fund, and you lose control over when to buy or sell the stocks that comprise your fund.

Ironically, some of the firms that offer folios and separate accounts are mutual fund companies. That's right. Companies like Fidelity Investments and American Century, among others, are enthusiastically pursuing "do-it-yourself" mutual fund programs. These firms have folio programs in place that give you the tools to create your own personal portfolio for a lot less than you'd pay to invest in one of their traditional mutual fund programs. Discount brokerage firms like E*Trade and Quick & Reilly have joined the folio fray as well in recent years.

Why all the pushing and shoving from the financial services folks? Because they believe the personal portfolio market is too huge to ignore.

- Fact: The personal portfolio (or separate accounts) market is growing by about 30 percent annually, according to Cerulli Associates.
- Fact: By 2004, it will be a $1.2 trillion market, according to the Money Management Institute, up from $425 billion in 1999.
- Fact: According to the firm Separate Account Solutions, about $1 trillion (one quarter of mutual fund assets) will be flowing to private fund portfolios in the next decade.
- Fact: They will soon be available just about anywhere, including banks, online brokers, full-service brokers, insurers, securities clearing firms, mutual fund companies, and credit unions.

Right now the largest purveyor of "build your own mutual fund" programs is a company called FOLIO*fn*. This company was founded by venture capitalist Steve Wallman in order to create a new investment vehicle that was essentially a blend of a mutual fund and a discount brokerage. In 2000, FOLIO*fn* opened its doors and rolled out the industry's first "build your own mutual fund" programs.

Wallman's "folios" are pretty much the industry standard for a standardized method of opening and managing your own personal mutual fund. Another company—called Sharebuilder.com—offers a new twist on the do-it-yourself mutual fund craze. Sharebuilder offers a program called Plan Builder that enables you to determine your investing style and risk tolerance based on your answers to four multiple choice questions. Once you answer the questions, Sharebuilder will recommend an asset allocation blueprint for building your own personal portfolio. Then the company offers a list of stocks that fits that custom-styled asset allocation blueprint. Once you select the stocks you like—voilà! You have your own mutual fund.

Companies Currently Offering "Do-It-Yourself" Mutual Fund Programs

FOLIO*fn*

Though only founded in 1997, FOLIO*fn* (*www.FOLIO fn.com*) is the granddaddy of all the folio firms. It allows you to build your own mutual fund portfolio of anywhere from one to fifty stocks. It also allows you to buy and sell more stocks for your portfolio anytime you want, with a whopping 500 commission-free trades every month. The service costs $295 per year. The company is working arm-in-arm with the mutual fund industry in cutting deals and forging partnerships to provide more folio options for its customers. The firm also has a cool feature called "Watch Accounts." These are sample accounts you can build (with no real money traded) to get you accustomed to trading and moving around the site. It's sort of a dress rehearsal for the do-it-yourself investing set.

BuyandHold.com

Recently bought out by Freedom Investments, BuyandHold.com *(www.buyandhold.com)* is a boon to long-term investors who want to take their time building their own financial portfolios and are in no rush to sell. The company offers access to its portfolio-building programs for only $6.95 per month, with no account minimums. Two free trades a day are thrown into the mix as well, as is a "personalized" stock tracker that follows your investments every day for you.

Sharebuilder.com

Billed as the "online broker for long-term investors," Sharebuilder.com *(www.sharebuilder.com)* has made a big dent in the retail investor market, with its low-cost $12 per month fees, no account minimums, no inactivity fees, and easy-to-follow automatic investment plans. Even if you don't subscribe, Sharebuilder still allows you to buy stocks for your own mutual fund at $4 per trade. Careful, though—that's only if you're buying stocks. If you sell stocks through Sharebuilder, the price goes up to $15.95. Ouch.

FreeTrade

A division of Ameritrade, FreeTrade *(www.freetrade.com)* is more of a discount brokerage service than it is a pure folio company like FOLIO*fn*. That said, it offers cheap trading fees (your first twenty-five stock trades each month are free; after that, trades are billed to you on a sliding scale from $1 to $3 per trade, depending on how many trades you make). The company also offers a real-time streaming data feature for $9.99 per month and a real-time news-ticker for $29.99 per month.

Brokerage America

Another discount brokerage company, right? But if you lift the veil, you'll see that Brokerage America *(www.broker ageamerica.com)* has entered the folio market with a "basket trading" feature that allows you to build a portfolio of stocks for about $5 per stock (up to ten stock trades per month). The company also offers some help with a mathematical model feature that recommends the best stocks for your personalized mutual fund.

E*Trade

The home of the $9.99 trade execution, E*Trade *(www.etrade.com)* has also waded into the personal portfolio market with a slew of stock baskets and portfolio tracking programs for do-it-yourselfers. E*Trade enables you to build your own mutual fund, letting you choose from up to fifty stocks per portfolio. It charges much as a traditional financial advisor does for the stock basket service, with fees from 0.75 to 1.25 percent of total portfolio value on an annual basis. That's still lower than what you'd pay for a traditional non-index mutual fund.

Portfolio Builder

Portfolio Builder *(www.portfolio.net)* offers a fresh look at the portfolio planning game, giving investors a chance to buy dollar amounts—instead of share amounts—of publicly traded companies and then tracking them for you in your own fund portfolio. Fees are either $11.95 per month or $3.99 per trade. No minimum balance, either.

Folios versus Mutual Funds

Whether you work with a FOLIO*fn* or a Sharebuilder.com (or any other folio provider) as "caretakers" for your self-styled mutual fund, you can expect some differences between folios and mutual funds. Here's a snapshot:

• Ownership—Folios enable investors to take direct ownership in the companies whose stocks they buy. That's not the case with mutual funds, which are investment vehicles registered with the Securities and Exchange Commission. That means while you may own shares of the fund, you don't own shares of the company. With folios, investors take direct ownership in the company, complete with full voting rights at company shareholder meetings.

• Control—Some folks don't want anything to do with the management of their financial portfolios. That's perfectly fine—mutual funds are a good way to provide investors with professional money management (although some argue that service comes at a stiff financial price). While some folios, like the ones offered by Fidelity, Morgan Stanley, and some of the larger investment advisory firms, come with a financial advisor option (meaning you can get financial advice on which stocks to buy for your fund from a registered financial planner), "pure" folios give you *all* the control over which stocks to buy or sell and when to buy or sell them.

• Taxes—With mutual funds, control over your tax picture is pretty much nonexistent. Since mutual fund managers decide when to sell stocks in the fund, thus determining a fund-holder's liability for capital gains and losses, that means you—as the fund-holder—are stuck with the resulting tax bill. That bill is passed on to fund shareholders in the form of a taxable distribution. With folios, you control when stocks are bought and sold, and the resulting tax liability of any dividends or capital gains or capital loss events. Consequently, you control your tax situation.

A Look at Folios

Personal portfolios—or "folios" for short—provide many of the same benefits of mutual funds:

- Diversification—Most folio programs allow you to choose from up to fifty different stocks for your account.
- Ease of use—There's no big mystery in signing up for a folio. Just go online at one of the folio providers' Web

sites, take a minute to complete some paperwork, and off you go.

- Index investing—Many folios are cut from the "Ready to Go" cloth. So if it's a Standard & Poor 500 Index you want, or a Dow Jones Industrial Average index fund, you can easily obtain them with folios.

That said, folios transcend what mutual funds offer in other key areas:

- Customization—You can build your own folio pretty much any way you want—to fit your specific financial needs and goals.
- Taxes—Folios provide you with more control over your tax liability than do funds.
- Fund tracking—The Internet makes it easy to track the performance of your folios, check on recent trades, and adjust your folio for ever-changing financial events, like a marriage, a new house, or maybe your twins going off to college.

What Are Folios?

Folios are the NASCARs of Wall Street, custom-built to ensure maximum power, control, and performance for their owners. Proponents bill them as the best of both worlds—investment vehicles that blend the simplicity and diversification of mutual funds, with the control of individual stock ownership.

Essentially, folios are personalized baskets of stocks and/or bonds that you buy on your own through a folio provider like FOLIO*fn* or Sharebuilder.com. Unlike with a mutual fund, where the stocks are owned by a group of investors, you, as the owner of your folio, are the owner of all the stocks that comprise your portfolio.

Typically, folios enable do-it-yourself investors to buy a basket of up to fifty or so stocks that can be purchased with a single transaction or through multiple transactions. Unlike individual stock investments, folios give you instant diversification. Unlike mutual funds, folios allow you to directly own individual stocks.

Most folio companies have a deep roster of stocks to choose from. FOLIO*fn*, for example, offers a menu of 3,500 stocks for you to peruse and select from. And it's not just stocks, either. Folio firms like Quick & Reilly and FOLIO*fn* also offer customers the option to buy other types of securities, such as exchange-traded funds, real estate investment trusts, and bond funds—a well-struck blow for investment diversity.

But going solo is a popular option as well with folio providers. Although FOLIO*fn* offers its customers about seventy-five "ready-made" folios (so if you're into international stocks they have an international folio that fits your investment profile; the same with energy stocks or large company stocks), it also enables you to build your own fund.

With unlimited trading included in the $295 annual fee that FOLIO*fn* offers, you can save a bundle if you're adding and subtracting stocks from your fund on an active, regular basis. For example, if you were to pay $10 per trade, as you would at E*Trade and many other online discount brokers, forty trades per year would cost you $400 annually in commission costs. But with a flat-fee folio provider like FOLIO*fn*, forty trades (or fifty or sixty and so on) would only set you back the original $295 you laid out as your annual fee for signing up.

Folio providers have "play lists" of ready-made model portfolios to choose from, as well as model folios that you can invest in or modify to suit your needs. For example, you can choose a folio based on a major index, such as the Dow Jones Industrial Average. If you don't like every stock in the model portfolio, you can change it. Another example: Say you don't like that hard liquor company or tobacco company in the model portfolio your folio company has provided. All you have to do is e-mail or call them telling them to drop that particular (and personally offensive) stock from your portfolio.

"Ready to Roll" Portfolios

Most folio providers offer ready-made mutual fund portfolios. While the purpose of this book is to help you build your own mutual fund portfolio, it's nice to know you have this option. Here are some samples you can expect to see:

- Stock market folios—Dow Jones 30, Global Equity, Energy Company, Russell 2000.
- Asset class folios—Large-Cap Growth, Large Cap Value, Small Cap Value.
- Sector folios—Aerospace, Automotive, Biotechnology, Internet Services.
- Social issues folios—Tobacco-Free, Environmentally Responsible, Alcohol-Free. ❖

Sample Aerospace Industry Portfolio from FOLIO*fn*

# Symbol	Company	Weight (% of Folio)
1. AH	ARMOR HOLDINGS INC	3.33%
2. AIR	AAR CORP	3.33%
3. ATK	ALLIANT TECHSYSTEMS INC	3.33%
4. AVL	AVIALL INC NEW	3.33%
5. BA	BOEING CO	3.33%
6. BEAV	BE AEROSPACE INC	3.33%
7. COL	ROCKWELL COLLINS INC	3.33%
8. CW	CURTISS WRIGHT CORP	3.33%
9. DCO	DUCOMMUN INC DEL	3.33%
10. DRS	DRS TECHNOLOGIES INC	3.33%
11. EASI	ENGINEERED SUPPORT SYS INC	3.33%
12. EDO	EDO CORP	3.33%
13. ERJ	EMBRAER-EMPRESA BRASILEIRA DE SP ADR PFD	3.33%

Sample Aerospace Industry Portfolio from FOLIO*fn* (cont'd)

#	Symbol	Company	Weight (% of Folio)
14.	ESL	ESTERLINE TECHNOLOGIES CORP	3.33%
15.	ESLT	ELBIT SYS LTD ORD	3.33%
16.	FLIR	FLIR SYS INC	3.33%
17.	GD	GENERAL DYNAMICS CORP	3.33%
18.	GR	GOODRICH B F CO	3.33%
19.	IDE	INTEGRATED DEFENSE TECHNOLOGIE	3.33%
20.	LLL	L-3 COMMUNICATIONS HLDGS INC	3.33%
21.	LMT	LOCKHEED MARTIN CORP	3.33%
22.	MOG.A	MOOG INC CL A	3.33%
23.	NOC	NORTHROP GRUMMAN CORP	3.33%
24.	ORB	ORBITAL SCIENCES CORP	3.33%
25.	PCP	PRECISION CASTPARTS CORP	3.33%
26.	RTN	RAYTHEON CO NEW	3.33%
27.	SQAA	SEQUA CORPORATION CL A	3.33%
28.	TGI	TRIUMPH GROUP INC NEW	3.33%
29.	TTN	TITAN CORP	3.33%
30.	UIC	UNITED INDL CORP	3.33%

Source: FOLIOfn.

Questions and Answers

Sure, folios sound great, but you still may have some uncertainties about them. (This is not surprising, considering how relatively new a concept they are for most people.) Here are some questions and answers that may make things much clearer.

#1: Are Folios Right for Me?

Well, if you're reading this book, you're at least intrigued by the notion of creating your own custom-styled mutual fund.

But if you don't want direct control over your own invest-ments, don't consider yourself a good record-keeper, and can't trust yourself to keep a lid on trading costs (since you'll be the one making the trading decisions for your portfolio), then per-sonal portfolios may not be for you.

Ideally, if you've already invested in mutual funds and have a modest amount of money invested in them ($25,000 or higher, for example), personal portfolios could be a good idea. You're almost certainly going to do better, fee-wise. Experienced investors, even slightly experienced ones, know their way around a stock table and probably read *The Wall Street Journal*.

Correspondingly, if you are a beginner at the investing game, and have only accumulated $5,000 or $10,000 in investable assets, you may want to shy away from personal portfolios, at least for now. Your annual mutual fund fees probably will be lower at those dollar levels than the average folio annual fee.

#2: How Can I Open My Own Folio?

Start by contacting one of the firms described earlier. They'll either take your information over the phone or direct you to their Web site where you'll fill out a form (online) and likely answer a few questions on:

1. Your investment risk tolerance.
2. Your financial goals.
3. Your timeline for retirement.

The answers to these questions will give the folio com-pany a thumbnail sketch of what kind of investor you are. Once you create your folio account, you can fund it imme-diately by wiring money or sending funds through the mail. You can begin buying stocks for your fund once your folio account is funded.

#3: How Do I Buy Stocks with a Folio?

Most folio providers give you an option: You can log onto your folio company's Web site, enter your password, access your account, and begin buying stocks by stock symbol. For example, if you think Ford Motor Company or General Motors belongs in your personal mutual fund, simply type in "F" or "GM" and the amount of shares you want, and press the enter key. Note that with most folios, trades are executed in "market order" fashion—not "limit order" fashion. This means you get the price the stock is selling at near the time when you place your order. With limit orders, you set the price you want to buy or sell a stock. But with trading time restrictions, folio companies have found limit orders cumbersome and unwieldy. So market orders it is.

Another option is to use a folio provider's stock selector tool to buy your stocks. In this case, the folio will have a menu of stocks you can scroll through and highlight the ones you want to buy. The system takes care of the rest. A big advantage here is that you can use these stock selection tools to screen stocks according to their sector, market capitalization, price-to-earnings ratio, Wall Street analysts' estimates, earnings growth, and other measures.

#4: How Do I Customize My Folio?

Easy. If, for example, you want to assemble your mutual fund to resemble the thirty stocks in the Dow Jones Industrial Average, you can cherry-pick as many stocks in the index as you'd like—usually by opting for a "Ready to Go" folio that's already set up in your folio provider's system. For stocks you don't like or don't want that may be in the Dow Jones index, you can simply opt to keep it out of your folio by deleting it.

#5: Should I Use a Financial Advisor to Build My Own Mutual Fund?

Using a financial advisor is never a bad idea. A good financial planner can get you started in the right direction and is available to answer any questions or deal with any crisis that may come down the pike. Of course, the advice will cost you— probably about one percent of the value of your personalized mutual fund. But, if you're squeamish about reviewing your portfolio holdings, or unsure of your ability to hone in on specific investment strategies, there's nothing wrong with hiring an advisor to do it for you. Plus, many folio companies offer personal financial planning advice as part of their packages.

Mutual Fund Costs versus Folio Costs

Let's say you have $150,000 in several stock mutual funds. At fund management fees of, say, 1.5 percent, you're paying about $2,250 in annual fees.

If you go through a FOLIO*fn* or a PortfolioBuilder, you're going to come out way ahead, as far as fees go. Remember, FOLIO*fn* only charges you $295 per year.❖

#6: How Often Can I Trade the Stocks in My Folio?

It depends, as folio options vary from company to company. Some folio providers, like FOLIO*fn* and Quick & Reilly, allow you to trade only twice daily, at predetermined times. Others, like E*Trade and Brokerage America, offer trading whenever you want.

#7: Can I Roll My IRA Over into a Folio?

Sure. In fact, folio providers are going out of their way to make it easy for you to do just that. IRA asset classes you can roll over into your folio include:

- Traditional IRA
- Roth IRA
- Rollover IRA
- SEP IRA (Simplified Employee Pension)

Index Funds versus Folios

The Road Runner versus Wiley Coyote. The Concorde versus the Spirit of St. Louis. NASCAR versus an electric golf cart. Actively managed funds versus index funds.

Get the point?

When mutual fund firms saw that investors wanted an alternative to fast-moving, sometimes risky actively managed funds they decided to slow things down a bit and roll out funds that were easy to follow.

Thus the index mutual fund was born.

Officially introduced by Malvern, Pennsylvania–based Vanguard Group in the 1980s, but used by pension plan managers long before that, index mutual funds are designed to mirror the performance of the stock market, or a specific sector of the market, as measured by the appropriate benchmark index. In contrast, actively managed funds are just that—they're managed by a money manager paid to pick the best stocks available.

Index mutual funds basically guarantee that the fund's performance will match an index. For example, if you invest in a mutual fund that tracks a big index like the Standard & Poor's 500 or the Dow Jones Industrial Average, your fund will likely match the performance of those indexes over the course of a calendar year.

An index fund is composed of hundreds of stocks from different industries or sectors, thereby helping to limit the negative impact of a downturn in any single stock or sector (i.e., diversification, one of the cardinal rules of investing). Usually, they offer better performance than traditional mutual funds, although there hasn't been any official comparison between index funds and personal portfolios, at least from a performance standpoint. According to Standard & Poor's, on average, only 10 to 20 percent of mutual fund managers outperform the overall market, so an index fund that's able to approximately match the performance of the overall market will beat 80 to 90 percent of all mutual fund managers.

Investors, especially beginners, are attracted to index funds because the returns are relatively dependable, relying solely on the index performance and not the decisions of a portfolio manager. Investors also like index funds because they're easy to use. Since the index funds are attempting to mirror the indexes they cover, decisions are automatic and transactions are kept to a minimum. A bonus: Since decisions are easy to make, fund companies don't spend a lot of money on high-priced managers to choose stocks for you. Consequently, expenses tend to be lower than those of actively managed funds, although they're still higher than folios.

Conservative investors like index funds because they are, well, conservative. While no investor is thrilled at the prospect of a severe market downturn, index funds have a built-in "middle of the road" mechanism that keeps them from investing in riskier securities. Of course, that means over time, you may miss out on big market upswings and hot stock sectors because index funds usually shy away from higher-risk stocks.

So, are index funds for you? They are if you're the type of investor who:

- Doesn't want a lot of investment risk.
- Likes to keep fees and administrative costs low.
- Doesn't want your investments to be overly complicated.
- Wants to keep your fund's tax liability low.

Index funds are not for you if you're the type of investor who:

- Prefers the stock-picking prowess a good fund manager can provide.
- Wants better than average fund returns—and can accept the accompanying risk that comes with actively managed funds.
- Likes the drama and action that index funds invariably don't provide.

Still not sure? Talk it over with a financial advisor. He or she can help you decide whether or not you're an investor who thrives in the fast lane or relaxes in the slow lane.

A Sample Portfolio Investment

#	Symbol	Company	Price/Share	Shares	Weight (% of Folio)	Total Price
1	AA	ALCOA INC	$29.625000	5.62647	1.67%	$166.68
2	AXP	AMERICAN EXPRESS CO	$55.500000	5.62647	3.12%	$312.27
3	BA	BOEING CO	$59.562500	5.62647	3.35%	$335.13
4	C	CITIGROUP INC	$51.000000	5.62647	2.87%	$286.95
5	CAT	CATERPILLAR INC DEL	$33.375000	5.62647	1.88%	$187.78
6	DD	DU PONT E I DE NEMOURS & CO	$44.625000	5.62647	2.51%	$251.08
7	DIS	DISNEY WALT CO	$41.375000	5.62647	2.33%	$232.80
8	EK	EASTMAN KODAK CO	$40.250000	5.62647	2.26%	$226.47
9	GE	GENERAL ELEC CO	$58.062500	5.62647	3.27%	$326.69
10	GM	GENERAL MTRS CORP	$59.687500	5.62647	3.36%	$335.83
11	HD	HOME DEPOT INC	$50.687500	5.62647	2.85%	$285.19
12	HON	HONEYWELL INTL INC	$36.437500	5.62647	2.05%	$205.01
13	HWP	HEWLETT PACKARD CO	$89.437500	5.62647	5.03%	$503.22
14	IBM	INTERNATIONAL BUSINESS MACHS	$114.875000	5.62647	6.46%	$646.34
15	INTC	INTEL CORP	$37.562500	5.62647	2.11%	$211.34
16	IP	INTL PAPER CO	$28.375000	5.62647	1.60%	$159.65
17	JNJ	JOHNSON & JOHNSON	$94.625000	5.62647	5.32%	$532.40
18	JPM	MORGAN J P & CO INC	$146.750000	5.62647	8.26%	$825.68
19	KO	COCA COLA CO	$58.187500	5.62647	3.27%	$327.39
20	MCD	MCDONALDS CORP	$29.937500	5.62647	1.68%	$168.44
21	MMM	MINNESOTA MNG & MFG CO	$93.125000	5.62647	5.24%	$523.96
22	MO	PHILIP MORRIS COS INC	$31.187500	5.62647	1.75%	$175.48
23	MRK	MERCK & CO INC	$76.875000	5.62647	4.33%	$432.53
24	MSFT	MICROSOFT CORP	$54.562500	5.62647	3.07%	$306.99
25	PG	PROCTER & GAMBLE CO	$72.437500	5.62647	4.08%	$407.57
26	SBC	SBC COMMUNICATIONS INC	$50.937500	5.62647	2.87%	$286.60
27	T	AT&T CORP	$26.750000	5.62647	1.51%	$150.51
28	UTX	UNITED TECHNOLOGIES CORP	$71.812500	5.62647	4.04%	$404.05
29	WMT	WAL MART STORES INC	$46.375000	5.62647	2.61%	$260.93
30	XOM	EXXON MOBIL CORP	$93.312500	5.62647	5.25%	$525.02
					100.00%	$10,000.00

A snapshot of a $10,000 investment in FOLIO*fn*'s FOLIO 30, which mirrors the Dow Jones Industrial Average.

Source: FOLIOfn; current as of October 5, 2000.

Case Study: *A Quick and Easy Start*

Opening his own personal portfolio account was easy for Rich Bowren, a professional triathlete and champion long-distance bicycle racer.

"I'd heard about folios from my financial advisor but I didn't think they were for me, originally," he says. "But when she explained to me how easy they were and how affordable I decided to give folios a try."

Rich found a folio company he liked and opened his account online in a matter of minutes. "I vetted the company through my planner and went right to work opening the account. I filled out some investment goals–type paperwork and they ran me through some sample portfolios to see what worked for me.

"Initially, I wound up taking one of the 'ready to go' portfolios that pretty much matched the small-cap growth mutual fund I had invested in. But after a week or two, as I felt more comfortable, I began replacing several of the small-cap growth stocks with some large-cap stocks like Cisco and Procter & Gamble for some stability."

Rich ran the selections by his financial advisor who approved.

"You know what was great? The moment my planner said to me, 'Congratulations, you've built your own mutual fund.' And it was all so easy, too."

Rich Bowren Personal Portfolio
ALLOCATION PERCENTAGES
35% value stocks
15% growth stocks
10% aggressive growth stocks
10% international stocks
30% Treasury bonds
FOLIO FAVORITES
Johnson & Johnson, General Electric, Hewlett-Packard

Chapter Checklist

✓ Buying twenty stocks from a discount broker can give you a mutual fund, but it's not really a folio, per se. It's more expensive than using a folio company and you have to keep track of the portfolio yourself.

✓ Exchange traded funds are a fine option, too, but they're not folios either. With these funds you get many of the same tax and fee advantages of folios—but not the customization.

✓ According to the firm Separate Account Solutions, about $1 trillion or one-quarter of mutual fund assets will be flowing to private fund portfolios in the next decade.

✓ FOLIO*fn*, BuyandHold.com, and Sharebuilder.com are the top folio providers. But banks, brokers, and even mutual fund companies are getting into the act with their own folio programs.

✓ Personal portfolios—or "folios" for short—provide many of the same benefits of mutual funds, including diversification, ease of use, and a broad array of investment options. They go beyond funds in also offering customization, tax breaks, and reduced fees.

✓ Opening a folio account is easy. You can be up and trading in as little as fifteen minutes.

Chapter 3

Taking Your Personal Financial Inventory

"Preparation is 90 percent responsible for what happens on Sunday. The rest is just three or four plays."
—BILL PARCELLS, PROFESSIONAL FOOTBALL COACH

There's an old joke about a guy on his hands and knees looking for some lost money on the street one night. A cop pulls up and asks the man what he's doing.

"I'm looking for twenty dollars I lost on Mulberry Street," the gent responds.

"But this is Maple Street," the cop answers.

"I know," says the man, still crawling along the pavement. "But the lighting's better here."

When it comes to managing our own money, many of us act like the guy who lost his money on Mulberry Street. We try to take the easy way out, common sense be damned. Whether it's the loudmouth day trader bragging about his big score that day, but who can't balance his checkbook, or the whack job down the block who stuffs his savings into a mattress "because it's a well-known fact that Martians actually run the banking industry," some people seem unable or unwilling to take the time to manage their money correctly.

Are you serious about taking control of your financial life? You see, it's no secret that paying closer attention to your personal financial situation will not only make it much easier to build your own supernova mutual fund, it is also one of the smartest moves you'll ever make. Sure, you might check your mutual fund every day, and you're always on the lookout for the next hot stock, but that's not what we're talking about—at least not yet, anyway.

No, this chapter is devoted to the philosophy that, in financial investing, as in most other instances in life, you have to walk before you can run. That's why knowing the financial basics—things like knowing your net worth, crafting a household budget, understanding the machinations behind credit and debt, and the importance of paying yourself first—are so important. These—and not the next biotechnology stock supernova—are the cornerstones of your own wildly successful mutual fund. Knowing the financial basics not only will give you a significantly greater sense of security, it will also give you a nice launching pad to dive into the fun stuff later on when you begin to build your own mutual fund. You know, things like picking off points on the NASDAQ market or buying Portuguese debentures on your laptop at 2 A.M. in your underwear.

Unfortunately, most people address their financial planning in ambiguous terms. They want their money to grow, and may measure performance against the stock market, but they don't look at what they really need to have happen. What's more, they don't consider the effects of spending and borrowing in concert with the positives of saving and investing.

So, in the spirit of that "walk first, run second" mantra I've been yammering away about, before you can strap on your mutual fund building boots it's imperative that you have your everyday financial life in order. Here's where to start.

Know Your Net Worth

In a global economy where information is as much a commodity as widgets or weed whackers, it pays to know what you're worth. While that goes for young and old alike, it's especially true for baby boomers, the oldest of whom turned fifty-four in 2000 and the youngest thirty-six.

That's where a *personal balance sheet* comes in handy.

A personal balance sheet gives you a blueprint for your financial life, one that you can work from again and again as you make lifetime financial decisions (and you can also use it when you are working on your mutual fund portfolio). It's a fluid document that you'll need to revisit every six months or (at the outer limits) every year. In any event, you'll be glad you have it. Quantifying your financial goals is critical in the whole self-created portfolio process, and your personal balance forms the yardstick by which you can measure the success of your financial plan. As time marches on, you can tweak the strategy for your financial plan along the way to achieve your defined goals.

What else can a personal balance sheet do for you? It won't cut your cholesterol or give you dimples, but it can help you calculate your net worth.

Calculating your net worth is the first step in planning for your own mutual fund. A net worth calculation can serve as a financial planning wake-up call, especially when the end result is a low or even negative number.

Defining "Net Worth"

Simply stated, your net worth is the difference between your assets and liabilities. Typically, *assets* include bank accounts, stocks, mutual funds, Individual Retirement Accounts or 401(k) plans, and other investments as well as the present value of a home, vacation home, car, and any other property that could be sold. You could also include money owed to you by others that you know you could receive and the value of your life insurance.

Liabilities are your debts and obligations. They should be divided into short-term debt (current bills, personal loans, credit card balances, etc.), and long-term debts (mortgages, other installment loans, etc.). You should also include any income taxes that would be owed, as well as any other obligations.

When you take a crack at your balance sheet, remember to include only what you have now; don't fudge the numbers because you expect a pay raise or bonus. In technology terms those are "vaporware" items—revenues that may or may not appear depending on the whims of your boss, Alan Greenspan, or Dionne Warwick's psychic hot line for all you know. Those as yet unrealized dollars don't factor into your net worth until you turn that money into an asset.

To be most accurate, you will also want to get a ballpark estimate of the market value of your home (which hopefully has gone up since you purchased it) and your cars (where the value has depreciated or gone down) and other major property items. You might try to get a ballpark estimate on the worth of everything, from your wardrobe to your books, televisions, stereos, jewelry, and other major possessions.

Debts come next, so total up the outstanding amount you owe on the mortgage, student loans, car loans, credit cards, money borrowed from relatives, and so forth. Exclude monthly bills for things such as the telephone, grocers, rent, and the like; they factor into your cash flow and could be slowing down how much money you pump into increasing your net worth, but they are not part of a snapshot of your personal wealth.

Once you subtract the debt from your assets, you'll have an interesting number. If it's positive, this is the amount of money you would be worth if you paid off your debts today.

But what makes net worth most interesting is looking at it on a regular basis, seeing how much it has grown or shrunk over the previous year. Charting your progress on net worth is important because many people increase both their assets and liabilities at the same time. They put money away into the company retirement plan, for example, while financing new cars or increasing credit card debt.

They may feel "better off," but it might be a mirage. If your net worth statement churns out a negative number, it tells you how big a hole you would be in if you were forced to liquidate everything to pay off your debts.

While any time of year is a good time to check out your personal balance sheet, a year-end analysis may be your best bet. While you are popping the cork on a vintage bottle of bubbly and wondering if Dick Clark has a time machine stashed away that the rest of us don't know about, you can knock off several financial tasks at once. Think about it. Since you're going to have to start compiling income and other records to do your taxes, why not check in with your portfolio and see how Junior's college fund is doing or how much of a mortgage payment you have left?

Six Easy Steps to Your Net Worth

Here's a simple formula to figure out your net worth. If your pencil's broken, keep in mind that most investment companies, like Fidelity, Putnam, and Merrill Lynch, offer online net worth calculation forms (and scores of other financial calculators, too) on their corporate Web sites.

1. List all of your fixed assets, such as real estate and cars, at their current value. Subtract any money that you owe on these assets, such as your mortgage or car loan.
2. List all of your liquid assets: cash, certificates of deposit, stocks, bonds, and bank accounts.
3. List all jewelry, furniture, and household items at their current value.
4. Add together all of the above. These are your total assets.
5. Subtract all of your debts (except those you already subtracted in step 1) from your total assets. The result is your net worth.
6. Re-evaluate and update your net worth calculations on an annual or, better yet, semi-annual basis.

Note: It is advisable to use the after-tax value of your marketable securities (stocks and bonds) when calculating their value.

Note II: If you arrive at a hefty net worth figure in your plus column, don't pump your fists skyward just yet. It's important to make sure the assets that make up your net worth are working in your favor for the long term. For example, bank savings won't keep up with inflation. That means your net worth may actually decline in real terms every year for people who place all their assets in a savings account.

Note III: If you're married or just living with that special someone, both spouses should take advantage of this planning exercise to learn something about the other spouse's business or profession. The whereabouts of business records, special business agreements, insurance policies, lease commitments on equipment or real estate, and the location of real estate deeds and mortgages should all be reviewed.

Make a List

When you do revisit your balance sheet, have a list of questions and/or checkpoints in mind to make your visit worthwhile. Try these for starters:

1. Has your net worth increased each year or since your last balance sheet? If it hasn't, you need to determine the reason and perhaps make some changes in your spending, saving, or other financial habits.

2. Does your balance sheet reflect a preference for personal assets such as an expensive home, cars, furs, and jewelry? Your balance sheet should show a concern for acquiring investment assets, not just personal assets that are far less likely to increase in value or produce income that will help you meet other financial goals.

3. Is your debt out of proportion? If your balance sheet shows excessive debt, especially for personal consumption, that's a signal to review your spending. Keeping debt under control is essential in good financial management.

4. Have you given enough thought to money needed for retirement? If your balance sheet shows total neglect for accumulating funds for retirement, you will want to make some changes as soon as possible.

5. Are your assets diversified? Diversification is a good hedge against inflation and changes in the economy. Having all your eggs in one basket is seldom a good idea. Also, don't keep excess cash in noninterest or low-interest accounts unless you have an immediate need for the cash.

6. Where do you want to be three years, five years, and ten years from now, in terms of your net worth? You might determine this by doing projected balance sheets for three years, five years, and ten years from now.

Hey, it's not rocket science. But a personal financial checkup every once in a while can come in handy when you're deciding what stocks or bonds should comprise your mutual fund and what your financial goals are in building your fund.

Don't Fret Debt

Some people treat personal debt like the plague, and they make a special effort to pay bills right away and keep their mitts off their credit cards. A few even accelerate payments on their mortgages, adding $50 or $100 each month to pay down their debt that much quicker. Bully for them—the money they save can be put to better use in the financial markets.

But just having debt, either a large amount or a small amount, doesn't make you a bad person. Like death, taxes, and your relatives, you can't really avoid debt—you can only manage it.

Besides, not all debts are bad ones. Using a mortgage to buy a home, tackling the rising costs of college with a loan, even borrowing money to buy a car—all are good debts with high return values. Home ownership, for example, provides a liquid asset and the interest on mortgage payments is tax deductible.

Where a savvy personal portfolio manager has to be careful is with the bad debt associated with high credit card use. Eating at a five-star restaurant or buying season tickets to watch the Cubs are worthwhile pursuits—*if* you can afford them with what you bring home in your wallet every payday. Using a credit card to finance these endeavors is a long-term loser, if only because most of the stuff you buy with credit cards depreciates rather than rises in value. Those high-top Nike basketball sneakers may look great in the box, but once you slap them on your feet, their value resides only in your mind's eye, because few others want them anymore. Unlike other depreciable items, like a car that provides vital transportation, or a pair of eyeglasses that allows you to see, most things you buy with a credit card don't offer much to your personal bottom line.

Building a Budget

If you want to get serious about building your own mutual fund, you're going to need money to invest in it. A great way to do that is to minimize debt. And the best way to minimize debt is to *manage* debt.

Let's start with a household budget. Without going through the ordeal of ranking your spending priorities, it is difficult to guarantee you will have anything left over at the end of the month to apply against your debts. If this sounds too taxing, then use the paperless budget method. Start by holding back a reasonable portion out of every paycheck to pay down your debts and force yourself to live on the balance.

If every now and then you come out ahead, be sure to apply your windfall to eliminate outstanding debts before you start to accumulate savings. This makes sense for a number of reasons. Borrowing rates typically exceed savings rates. Interest expense is usually nondeductible, whereas savings are taxable. Interest charges are a certainty, but investment returns are volatile.

Sure, creating budgets and paying off debts seems dry and boring. But let's face facts—it's not your father's economy anymore. In an era when consumer spending is high and when there are plenty of new goods and services to buy that weren't even available twenty years ago, knowing how to budget properly is a big key to your financial success. According to a recent American Express consumer survey on everyday spending, today's list of typical, day-to-day expenses is still dominated by traditional items such as groceries, fast-food lunches, tolls, and gasoline. But they've been joined by such twenty-first-century wallet sappers as cellular phone service, paging fees, and Internet service costs.

Consequently, as everyday expenses increase, managing a household budget becomes more complicated. The best solution? Get those costs into your budget as soon as possible. That's because people tend to spend whatever money is leftover after the fixed expenditures and stop only when either the ATM won't give them more cash or the bank calls.

One way to keep money from flying out of your pocket is to write down what you're spending as you spend it. You may not realize it, but that glass of Merlot after work, the dry cleaning you picked up on the way home, and that four-cheese pizza you had delivered to your door for dinner all add up. A record of your daily, weekly, or monthly expenditures makes for some interesting reading in most American households, testing the patience of millions of spouses in the process.

Some consumers like to use a credit card to buy everything (the credit card companies *love* to push that strategy). That way, at the end of the month, they have a ready-made laundry list of expenditures sent to them by their credit card firm. Bad idea. Sure, you get a nice, clean list of what you spent each month. But getting into the habit of using a credit card is never a good idea. It's easy to treat that Visa card like cash—but it ain't. Sooner or later you've got to pay for it, with high interest payments to boot if you're not on time every month. Besides, in the age of the laptop, it's easy to sit down at the end of the day and compile your own list. You'll have your record and you won't get sticker shock opening your credit card bill every month.

Your Budget Explained

Before we get into specific areas of your budget, let's take a brief look at how a normal household budget works.

Primarily, all budgets are divided into income and expenses, but most good ones now include a third component, savings. Items in the "income" section can include after-tax salary, pensions, investments, and tax refunds.

Items in the "expenditure" category can include rent, mortgage payments, food, gas, utility bills, childcare, entertainment, gifts, and holidays. The "savings" section logs how much you put away each month, after satisfying spending requirements. As much as 10 percent of total expenses should be put into this category to allow for unforeseeable events such as car repairs or dental emergencies or unemployment.

One way to attack your budget is to use what some debt counselors refer to as "the snowball method." Using this strategy, simply list your debts in ascending order with the smallest remaining balance first, the largest last. Do this regardless of interest rate or payment. You will pay these off in this new order. This works because you get to see some success quickly and are not trying to pay off the largest balance just because it has a high rate of interest.

Once you pay off the lowest balance, take that payment and combine it with the next payment on the list, so that each month you're making a larger payment on that debt. Repeat the process, again and again, so that your payments are getting larger, your debts are being paid off faster, and the process starts to snowball until all your debts are paid.

If you're one of those people who can't sleep at night worrying about bigger bills, go ahead and address those bills first. Just rank your debts in order of highest interest rate to lowest. Then whittle away at them in that order. Make sure you are not comparing apples and oranges. The effective interest rate is often different from the nominal rate quoted by the lender. For example, mortgage rates are compounded semi-annually, while rates on credit card debt are usually compounded monthly.

Your Budget List

Here are some more tips on building a better budget:

1. Don't make your budget too restrictive. Otherwise, you might lose the will to stick to it.

2. Use precise figures, not just estimates, so you know at any point exactly how much you need or have.

3. Consider using an Excel spreadsheet with two primary components—income and expenditure.

4. Budget sections should be easily understood. For example, include contractors and housepainters under Home Expenses. Better yet, paint the house yourself.

5. Don't underestimate what you spend. Figure in lunches that you eat in restaurants, movies (including "Pay-Per-View" at home), and other "extra" expenses.

6. Create and manage your budget on a monthly basis. Or build a budget that's based on how often you get paid.

7. Review your budget on a quarterly basis for accuracy—and to see how you're doing.

8. When the economy enters a low interest rate period, as it has in the last several years, take advantage of low interest rates to refinance a home mortgage and make lower monthly payments. Numerous Web sites offer instant calculators that will estimate your new payments, including *www.Quicken.com* and *www.realtor.com*.

9. Review auto and home insurance rates and comparison shop for better values. Some companies offer discounts you may not be aware of, such as those for senior citizens,

multiple policies, or autos with antitheft devices. Consider raising deductibles, too, in exchange for lower payments.

10. Add up the fees on your bank statements and shop for a better deal or ask your existing bank about lower-cost accounts. While you're at it, find out if your employer will automatically deposit your paycheck to your bank account to minimize the risk of bounced checks and other mishaps. Consider starting an automatic savings plan that will route some money directly to a separate account before you're tempted to spend it.

11. Obtain an estimate of your future Social Security income by calling 800-772-1213. Ask for a Personal Earnings and Benefits Statement request form. The response time is quick, and it's a good opportunity to make sure your employment history is reflected accurately.

12. Order a copy of your credit report for $8 from reporting agencies Equifax (800-685-1111), TransUnion (800-916-8800), or Experian (800-422-4879).

13. Get rid of clutter and raise extra cash by holding a garage sale, or get a tax deduction by donating unwanted items to charities. In that case, be sure to keep an itemized receipt of donated goods in case the IRS has questions.

14. Make a detailed household inventory to protect yourself in case of theft or disaster. Engrave your name and an identifying code on high-value items, and record serial numbers. Most insurance companies offer guidelines or even workbooks; call yours or check out the Nationwide Mutual Insurance Co. Web site at *www.nationwide.com*.

15. Taking out one manageable loan to pay off debts can often lower your cost of borrowing, particularly for credit cards. Interest rates on credit cards are usually much higher than traditional consumer loans.

16. Keep it fun. Open a bottle of wine, make a date with your loved one, flip a Dixie Chicks CD into your stereo. Saving money will put a smile on your face and make you feel good about yourself. It's time well spent.

Adding It Up

When you have filled in the sections of a budget table relevant to you, simply make totals of expenditure (including savings and investments) and income, and subtract expenditure from income. If your total is above zero, you are cash-flow positive. If the total is below zero, you are cash-flow negative. If the total is zero, you are cash-flow neutral.

If you end up with a positive cash flow, you can then consider investing the surplus, preferably in stocks or mutual funds. Or you can spend it. If you have a negative cash flow, you should examine what nonessential items you can eliminate.

The most common problem people have with budgets is sticking to them. Individuals who aren't very organized by nature need to have a more flexible budget, with broader categories such as "rent, entertainment, groceries, and bills" under expenses, rather than more detailed entries.

One last word on your budget. When you first start your budget, you should review it every pay period to see if you're on track. After that, review it when you do it—perhaps every month.

Pay Yourself First

When paying your bills each month, don't forget about number one. That's you, my friend.

So before paying your cell phone bill, or your cable bill, pay yourself first. After all, you have as much right to your money as anyone else. Paying yourself first doesn't mean allotting yourself some spending money right off the top for margaritas with the gang or a new Hermès scarf. Paying yourself first means giving you a chance to help your savings grow by putting some cash aside for your investments, as you do with a 401(k) or an Individual Retirement Account. It's no secret that progress toward financial independence can be accelerated significantly by putting your money to work for you.

Paying yourself first is the key to staying out of debt and keeping your financial house in order. Most folks don't practice this simple strategy because they believe they can't afford it. The fact is, they can't afford not to.

Cool Online Budgeting Tools

Online software is obviously a big help in managing your budget as well as your investment portfolio, but there are certain qualities that you should look for. For example, regular viewers of those business and money TV shows on cable hear a lot about budget software packages like Quicken or Microsoft Money. The reason? Both include household accounting functions in addition to their investment portfolio tools.

If you don't want to spend the $50 or so required to buy such a software package, there's always the Web. While the list of personal financial planning Web sites available runs long and deep, a few sites in general offer some stable budgeting and family finance advice.

Some sites I recommend include:

• **Quicken Financial Network** *(www.qfn.com)*—Easy to learn and easy to use. Does investment calculations in addition to budgeting. Plus, it has good tips and research sections.

• **FinanCenter** *(www.financenter.com/budget.htm)*—Fairly highbrow stuff. That said, the site has some cool calculators for figuring out your financial situation, particularly in the areas of budgeting and spending. The site has some good overall financial tutorials as well.

• **MetLife Online** *(www.metlife.com)*—The folks who brought you the Snoopy ads have a great site for everyday financial living. Just made a major purchase? The site has a financial calculator to help evaluate the financial impact on your life. The same story goes for major health expenditures—like surgery for a loved one in your family—or the impact of taking on a new job at a new salary.

- Kiplinger.com (*www.kiplinger.com*)—From the same folks who bring you *Kiplinger's* magazine, the company Web site has some good overall investment information in addition to its impressive roster of financial calculators.
- The Dollar Stretcher (*www.stretcher.com*)—A good site for the whole family. It has a great section on money and kids.

Crafting a Credit Card Strategy

Credit cards are a necessary evil, though often more evil than necessary. In many cases, the interest rate is 16 percent or more; the interest you pay is not tax-deductible; and quite often the money you owe is for something you've already gotten the use out of. Pay it off.

But first, make sure the credit card bill is accurate. Analyze the bill. Make sure it matches your receipts. Sometimes, when you sign on the dotted line, you don't double-check the amount of the purchase.

For example, amid the rush of holiday shopping, you might not have been charged the sale price for an item; you might have been charged twice for a single item; or you could even have been charged for an item purchased by someone else in line. It happens. If you notice a discrepancy, call your credit card issuer and dispute the charge.

Meanwhile, don't fall for any season's greetings from your credit card company offering to lower your minimum payment or saying that, because you're such a good customer, you can skip this month's payment. That sounds enticing, but remember, the interest-rate clock is still ticking.

With all your holiday shopping, in addition to your regular expenses, suppose that your January credit card bill is $2,500, a typical amount. If the annual interest rate is 18 percent, skipping January's payment could cost you about $38 in finance charges that will show up in next month's bill. No wonder the credit card company is so nice.

Monthly Budget Checklist

Here's a ready-made list for you to keep track of your monthly expenditures:

MONTHLY INCOME

Net monthly salary/wages	$
Net monthly income from interest and dividends	$
Other monthly income (e.g., family allowances and benefits)	$
Total Monthly Income	$
Living expenses	$
Rent/mortgage payments	$
Food and beverages	$
Utilities (e.g., electricity, water)	$
Clothing/footwear	$
Daily expenses (e.g., lunch)	$
Household expenses	$
Insurance (e.g., house and contents, life, health, car)	$
Health care	$
Personal care (e.g., pharmacist, hairdresser)	$
Medical (e.g., doctor, dentist, optician)	$
Transportation	$
Gasoline	$
Repairs and maintenance	$
Registration, license, service clubs	$
Public transport, taxis, parking	$
Other	$
Children's expenses	$
Recreation (e.g., sports and activities)	$

MONTHLY INCOME

Entertainment (e.g., dining out, movies, books)	$
Education (e.g., courses, associations)	$
Gifts (e.g., presents, donations)	$
Credit/loan repayments	$
Credit cards/charge account repayments	$
Rentals, hire purchase	$
Personal loan repayments	$
Savings and investments	$
Unexpected events, replacements, and additions	$
Savings, special goals, holidays, etc.	$
Investments in shares, properties, etc.	$
Total Monthly Expenditure	$
Total Monthly Income	$
Total Monthly Expenditure	$
Cash-flow Position +/-	$ +/-

First, Build a Personal Finance System

Planning for your long-term financial future isn't a 100-yard dash—although you wouldn't know it by the laser-like focus we direct to the stock market on a daily basis—but rather a marathon.

Consequently, we have to take a champion marathoner's mindset as we build the financial foundations that will support us throughout our lives. That means getting in good fiscal shape so we can tackle our personal financial portfolios head-on.

Part of that preparation is calculating your net worth, building a budget, and creating a personal balance sheet—things we've talked about already.

The second half of the preparation phrase is what we'll discuss for the rest of this chapter—organizing your personal financial records, figuring out how much you have to save for retirement, and then creating a financial blueprint that will secure your financial future.

We know, we know. There's no glamour or cachet in keeping tabs on your tax documents or calculating how much cash you'll need when you turn ninety. But as any Olympic marathoner will tell you, the race isn't won on marathon day. It's won in the preceding weeks and months when the real heavy lifting takes place—the road training, the diet, the mental preparation.

It's the same story in the personal portfolio game. How can you expect to take advantage of currency fluctuations in the Pacific Rim or risk arbitrage trends in the global steel industry if you can't manage to find the deed to your house? How can you know which funds to pick if you don't know how much money you'll need to live on in retirement? To truly benefit from the immense opportunities available in the financial markets, you just have to be prepared and stake out a plan as to where you want to go.

Getting Organized

Isn't it amazing that in the workplace, some people are organizational tigers, closing deals and creating new profit centers because they were prepared to take advantage of business opportunities?

Yet ask these corporate go-getters where their tax records are stored or how much money is in their 401(k) plan and in return you'll get a blank stare that practically demands the installation of a drool bucket on the go-getter's chin.

Why the lapse when it comes to personal financial records? Although it's not always clear, there's a school of thought that says people are reluctant to look at a tax form if it's not April 15, or a 401(k) form if the market's gone south for a few weeks. Or how about the "procrastination" theory, where an individual looks at the stack of paperwork teetering on her dining room table at the end of a long day and says "Oh, I'll get to it later—Penn & Teller are on *Letterman* tonight."

Who really knows? The "personal" in personal finance isn't there by accident. People have their own reasons for managing their financial affairs the way they want to, and—right or wrong—they deserve the final say in the money management decisions they make.

That said, failing to organize your personal financial records is a missed opportunity at best, and a potential IRS nightmare at worst. Organizing your financial documents can help you get more out of your money. Once you're organized, you can do a better job sticking to a budget and getting the most from your investments. Keeping track of bills, credit card receipts, and other financial documents also can help protect you from identity theft.

More specifically, if your financial documents aren't handy, how can you buy that 1,000 shares of Internet stock without knowing where it fits in your portfolio? Or what the tax ramifications might be? Or what if you get one of those ubiquitous letters from Uncle Sam saying the IRS would like to take a look at your tax returns for the past three years. Not having your records available is simply inviting trouble.

Are You Prepared for the Worst?

Few people invite trouble, but sometimes it comes knocking anyway. To get an idea of whether you might qualify for your own merit badge for being financially prepared, see how many of these "what-if" questions you can answer:

1. If you're hit with an unexpected large expense—the refrigerator died, your car brakes failed, a rotted tree in your yard has to go—how would you pay for it?

2. If your spouse died tomorrow, would you know how much money is available for you to carry on, including life insurance, investments, and savings? Would you know to whom you owe money?

3. If you were sued for $3 million, what would you do?

4. If you lost your job this week, do you have a backup plan? What if you were injured and couldn't work for one year?

5. If your parent suffered a debilitating stroke or other life-threatening illness, what action would you take? How would medical or nursing home expenses affect your own finances?

6. If your children want to attend an Ivy League university, how would you pay for it?

7. Finally, for your own financial peace of mind, how much money would you need to accumulate for you to say, "I have enough"?

The key to answering those questions, of course, is to plan ahead so that you can respond quickly and effectively should these hypothetical situations become reality. To make things easier, experts advise setting aside an emergency fund to ward off big bills. Make sure you have adequate insurance—life, health, disability, and liability. Know as much as you can about your finances—income, savings, and debts. And put together a team of financial advisors who can help you to make it through difficult times.

Creating a System

Fear not—organizing your financial records is as easy as it is well worth the effort.

First, let's define a spending record. For anyone trying to live on a budget or simply make a reasonable savings plan, a spending record is a low-tech self-examination of cash flow. It is different from budgeting because a spending record merely tracks the money you spend without making any attempt to allocate it. Budgeting, therefore, is a secondary part of the process.

Unlike a budget, a spending record by itself does not require a significant change in how a consumer uses money. Instead, the big change most often is a notebook, and the time it takes to write down all expenditures.

Most experts say it takes about a month to get a good handle on where the money is going, although a reasonable cash-flow estimate can be constructed by following the money for a week.

Where do you start? These days, just about everyone has a separate room in the house, or at least in the corner of the bedroom or the dining room, with a desk, maybe a personal computer, and some space to pay bills and conduct his or her personal business. If you open your mail in the kitchen, keep a file drawer handy. If you have a home office, get an inbox for bills and other personal mail. The key is not the sophistication of the space, but just having a dedicated place to handle your bills, your paperwork, and your money. Experts say a well-set-up work area or home office can help just about everyone reduce stress, improve productivity, and add more personal time to your day.

More and more people are turning to multitask computer programs like Quicken or Microsoft Money that automatically remind them of the bills to be paid, handle the math calculations, and make money management almost a pleasure. Plus, if you have both a computer and a modem, you can link your financial software to online services that let you keep track of your spending online. American Express cardholders, for example, can go to the Web site at *www.american express.com/cards* to review recent charges, check balances, view their Membership Rewards points, download transactions into Quicken or Microsoft Money, and even pay their bills. A PC-based personal finance software package also eliminates what the American Bankers Association confirms as the single largest reason people overdraw their checking accounts: math errors. That's because money management software makes calculating balances a no-brainer even for those who aren't math experts.

Unfortunately, the personal computing era has done little to back up its claim as the gateway to the "paperless" era. Even with significant gains in the area of online bill payment and electronic trading and banking, paper documents in the form of bills, invoices, trade confirmations, and the like are still very much with us, and they will be until the day consumers finally demonstrate a wholesale trust and commitment to electronic-based personal finance. With the proliferation of computer bugs and viruses, particularly through the Internet and through e-mail programs, that day isn't coming anytime soon.

In the meantime, organizing your paper documents is a must. You can start by keeping all of your essentials in one spot. Keep the most frequently used items—stamps, envelopes, stationery, file folders, and note pads—within arm's reach on your desk. If possible, place bookshelves and filing cabinets nearby. Create an inbox for mail and a "To File" box. Post a running supply list to refer to when replenishing your stock.

Then, go through all your financial records. Throw out all the records that you no longer need, like old credit card statements, pay stubs, and ATM receipts that are more than a year old. Throw away the payment books from loans that are now paid off, including your car. Toss expired guarantees and warranties, and instruction manuals from items you've discarded or sold. You can also throw away most mutual fund statements you receive: Keep only the consolidated annual report, which has a record of all the transactions from the year.

Be practical. Some papers are stored just for sentimental reasons. Ask yourself what's the worst thing that could happen if you threw it away. If absolutely necessary, could you get another copy? If you really want something for just sentimental reasons, transfer it to your scrapbook or cedar chest.

Shred the papers you plan to throw away. Your old personal papers are gold mines of information for thieves who may want your Social Security number or account numbers.

Keeping Track

After you have thrown out your old financial records, develop a filing system for the ones you keep. Here's a short list of the documents you're going to have to hang on to for a while:

- **Tax returns**—The Internal Revenue Service has three years from the time you file to audit you. But if you've underreported your income by 25 percent or more, the IRS has six years to challenge your returns. And there's no statute of limitations on investigations of taxpayers who fail to file or who file fraudulent returns. So to be safe, keep copies of your tax returns and supporting documents, such as receipts for charitable contributions and miscellaneous deductions, for at least six years.

- **Investment records**—If your mutual fund company or broker provides a year-end summary statement of your transactions, you can toss the monthly reports. Just make sure you have some record of all your trades, particularly purchases. That way, you'll have the original price of your stocks or fund shares when you sell (i.e., the basis), which will determine how much you owe in taxes. Also keep trade confirmations for a couple of years after you sell stocks or fund shares in case the IRS has questions. And save records of all contributions to a nondeductible IRA. That way, you'll have proof that you already paid taxes on the money when it comes time to start taking distributions. Otherwise, you may end up being taxed twice.

- **Credit card bills and bank statements**—Visa and MasterCard have advised customers to review their credit card statements for potential duplicate charges. Some merchants failed to upgrade their computer software for 2000, which can affect both credit and debit cards. Even if you don't find any errors, you may want to hold on to your credit card bills for a few months as a precaution. The same goes for your bank statements.

- **Deductions**—Charity receipts, church donations, etc.
- **Medical records**—Receipts and insurance payments for dentist, doctors, hospitals, and prescriptions.
- **Home records**—The deed to your house, your property tax paperwork, receipts for home repairs, warranties, etc.
- **Vital statistics**—Passports, birth certificates, marriage, and divorce papers.

Note: Never discard credit card receipts or other account numbers in a public trashcan. You can buy a bare-bones paper shredder for less than $50, and it's worth the money. Shredding old bills and bank statements will ensure they don't fall into the hands of dumpster divers who troll for credit card and Social Security numbers.

File It Away

After you earmark the documents you'll need, file them. Make a separate folder or file for each topic (e.g., bank account, loans, credit cards, taxes) so that each item is easy to file and find. After you have separated your records, put the folders in a storage file that is easily accessible.

Set up a monthly budget and schedule. Unless you pay each bill as it arrives, set time aside either monthly or twice a month to pay your bills. If you use a money management program, you can set it up to provide automatic reminders of the bills due. Otherwise, use a simple file folder and an index card file: Put the due dates and bills on index cards, and file them by the due dates. This will help you remember to pay your bills on time, avoiding service or late charges.

Balance your checkbook and charge statements each month. Go through the monthly checks you wrote, ATM receipts, and any other direct deposits/withdrawals from your account. Compare the amounts on your charge statement with your receipts. Notify the bank that issued the credit card of any errors as soon as possible. Federal law provides protection from mistakes only if you make notification within sixty days.

How Long to Keep Vital Documents?

Just like a can of onion soup, there's an expiration date on your critical financial documents. Some you keep for a year; some you keep a lot longer. Here's a snapshot of how long to hang on to the important stuff:

- Old credit card statements, pay stubs: one year
- Bank statements, canceled checks: three years
- Income tax returns: six years
- Home improvement records: ownership plus seven years
- Investment records (IRAs, pensions, insurance policies, etc.), real estate records and transactions, stock records, personal records (birth certificates, military, marriage/divorce, adoption, custody agreements, naturalization papers): permanently ❖

Here are some more tips to help you get fiscally fit:

- Cut down to one charge card per adult, two if you use one for home and one for work. This reduces statements and bill-paying time.
- Consolidate your bank accounts, if you have several.
- If you can, pay bills by automatic deduction. Most utility bills can be handled this way.
- Cut down junk mail by contacting the Direct Marketing Association at the Web Site *www.dmaconsumers.org/con sumerassistance.html* and ask them to remove you from their

direct mail lists. Or write to them at: Mail Preference Service, Direct Marketing Association, P.O. Box 9008, Farmingdale, NY 11735-9008.

• Consider getting professional help. Your financial management includes day-to-day living, estate planning, and tax strategies. This means you need a budget, a will, possibly a trust, and tax advice. If you don't know where to start, consider a consultation with a financial planner to get you started.

Setting Your Long-Term Financial Goals

Okay. The underpinnings are in place. Now it's time to start pouring the concrete.

With a renewed commitment to a personal budget, a handle on your net worth, and a new attitude about handling your personal financial records, it's time to get serious about where you want to be financially and how you plan to get there.

Whether it's a one-year plan to pay for your daughter's wedding, a ten-year plan to pay for your son's college education, or a thirty-year plan to save for retirement, establishing finite financial goals down the road a piece is a winner.

Achieve most of your goals—or come close—and you have measurable proof that you are headed in the right direction. Fall short, and it's a wake-up call that more drastic steps may be necessary.

Unfortunately, we're seeing more of the latter these days. A recent survey by a Big Four accounting firm shows that unless we save a great deal more than we currently do, three out of four Americans over the age of twenty will have less than half the money they need to retire and maintain their pre-retirement standard of living.

In fact, on average they would have to reduce their expenses by 60 percent—or get a job flipping burgers—in order to make it through their twilight years without running out of money.

If your after-tax expenses currently run $50,000 a year and you retire today, you would have to cut your spending by at least $30,000 if you want your money to last as long as you do. And that huge cut in your budget assumes that you have the good sense to die on the day you spend your last penny. If you survive longer than the actuaries estimate, you'll outlive your money.

That's why setting long-term financial goals is so critical. Fortunately, it's also pretty easy.

Here are some ideas that will help you establish your game plan:

1. Be specific. Aim for clear targets such as "$2,000 into a retirement account," rather than generalities like "contribute to savings."

2. Put pay raises directly into savings or toward debt reduction. If you can make ends meet now, then you don't need to live off the cash you get in a pay raise. That being the case, put the extra money where it will do the most good, either increasing retirement savings or trimming debt. In this way, you maximize the good of the pay raise and move toward long-term goals without reducing your standard of living.

3. Invest in stocks. It is virtually impossible to beat inflation and generate a decent return without investing in the stock market. You're taking on investment risk, but you are avoiding inflation risk, and if you have a diversified portfolio, you are spreading your investment risk. Inflation risk isn't to be understated, even though it's been relatively nonexistent for the past several years. Let's say you're heavily invested in Treasuries that pay 6 percent interest. Inflation suddenly spikes upward to 10 percent, and you're now losing money. The only way to compensate is to sell those investments at a loss and reinvest the money, or to continue falling further behind in real income because inflation is outstripping the return on your investments. (We'll have much more on stock investing throughout the book.)

4. Estimate how much you'll need to retire in comfort. Start with a rough estimate based on what you earn now. If you expect a more modest life in retirement, use 60 to 70 percent of your current income. However, if the future holds too many unknowns, start with 100 percent. Then tackle more detailed financial calculations—either on your own or with the help of financial planners—to assess such factors as the likely impact inflation will have on your purchasing power.

5. Develop a savings plan. How far away you are from retirement plays a large part in how you should invest your retirement money. Historically, there are three stages to a long-term regular savings plan for retirement: *capitalization, consolidation,* and *conservation.* In the first stage, you should be most concerned with building up your retirement savings portfolio. Take as aggressive an outlook as your nerves can stand because at this point there is little capital to risk. The second step, consolidation, makes up the bulk of your savings plan; balance the aggressive investments with some tamer ones to better protect your existing assets. The final change, from consolidation to conservation, when your investments should aim to preserve the capital you have, should take place one to three years before you retire. The exact timing of all these should take current market conditions into account.

6. Start saving now. You'll need to save enough from your thirty-odd years of working to live for about twenty years in retirement. So get cracking. When you do ramp up your savings program, overestimate your needs. It's far better to end up with too much money than not enough. Even a little bit more a year can make a difference in the long term.

7. Get some good life insurance. Solid life insurance is critical to your family's fiscal fitness. If you're out of commission, or worse, chances are you may not have enough life insurance to protect your loved ones. Usually, several hundred thousand dollars' worth of term life is the way to go. Term is generally the most inexpensive way to insure a life.

The policies offer no savings feature, no cash value, no retirement benefits. If the policyholder dies during the coverage period, the company pays a specified sum of money to the beneficiary. The key for deciding how much insurance to purchase is for each partner to determine how much money he or she would need to live comfortably.

Take Inflation into Account

When you begin planning your own mutual fund, take inflation into account. Inflation averages about 3 percent annually. At that rate, prices will double in twenty-four years. For example, today's $25,000 car will cost about $50,000 in twenty-four years, about $37,500 in twelve years, and about $31,250 in six years. ❖

How Much Should I Save for Retirement?

Things have changed a lot in 200 years or so. About the same time George Washington was leading his troops across the Delaware River to fight the British Army, the average life expectancy was only twenty-three years. By the time of the first World War, average life expectancy rose to forty-seven years of age. Fast forward to 2003, where the average American women lives to about eighty-two and the average American man to about age seventy-eight. In addition, the fastest growing segment of our population is the 100-plus crowd. These life expectancies are a big part of why we need to plan.

Consider something as basic as food. According to financial planner Ric Edelman in his *New York Times* bestselling book *The Truth About Money*, assuming you and your spouse retire at sixty-five and live to your normal life expectancy of eighty-five, you're going to eat 43,800 meals in retirement. That's three meals a day, 365 days a year over twenty years, for two people. If each meal costs $5, you'll spend $219,000 on food. Where is that money going to come from?

The good news is there's a simple way to figure out how much you'll need to retire on. First, you need to know how much you're spending today to maintain your lifestyle and then carry the numbers forward, adding a bit of inflation, to see what you'll need down the road. For example, if you are forty and want to retire at sixty, you have twenty years until retirement. Assuming you could live well on $50,000 annually, and plugging in a moderate 3 percent inflation rate, you'll need about $90,000 per year by the time you retire.

In general, the rule of thumb is having about 80 percent of your preretirement income to live on in retirement. But a better idea is to count on having 100 percent on hand. Inflation could go higher, Social Security may collapse, or you may live long enough so health care is a major, and expensive, issue.

How Much You Need to Retire Calculator

You're going to need a lot of money to live as well as you want to in retirement, especially since, thanks to healthful lifestyles and advanced medical technology, many Americans can expect to live into their nineties and even past 100. Here is how to determine how much you will need.

Current gross annual income:	$
Minus: amount of annual savings	$
Subtotal: what you currently spend	$
Times (x) .75%	$
Current standard of living (the amount you need to live on right now)	$
Times (x) inflation factor (5 years to retirement = .03%; 10 years = .037%; 15 years = .047%; 20 years = .058%)	$
Estimated annual living expenses in retirement =	$

The Advantages of Starting Early

The sooner you begin investing, the longer you should benefit from the compound interest earned on your personal portfolio. Consider two investors. One saves $2,000 a year for ten years between ages twenty-five and thirty-four. The other starts to save at age thirty-five and continues saving $2,000 a year through age sixty-five. Assuming an average annual return of 9 percent, the first saver would have $545,344 and the second would have $352,427. The difference? About $190,000 (or about the price of a nice beach house down in Florida). ❖

What Else Should I Consider Before I Start?

Retirement may not be your only financial goal as you continue to invest and beef up your portfolio. You may want to quit your job and start your own business. You may want to buy a vacation home. You may want to go back to college.

Who knows? Life offers up opportunities when we least expect them. So if a friend offers you a chance to manage your own pub in Ireland or if you get the chance to sail around the world, that's great. But only if you're in a position to pay for it.

One thing's for sure. The longer you keep your money in your portfolio working for you, the more money you'll accumulate for whatever goal or opportunity that is out there waiting for you.

Let's say that you have invested $100 that is compounded at 10 percent per year. Here's what you can expect to happen:

Year 1: $110
Year 2: $121
Year 3: $133
Year 50: $11,739

After one year, your investment only gains a measly ten bucks. But look what happens when you give your investment a real chance to grow? After fifty years, you've earned quite a bundle. The moral of the story? The longer you keep your money invested, the bigger your total return will be.

It gets better the sooner you start. Sure, they say life begins at forty. But saving for retirement should have started long before that—if you believe all those retirement planning books and articles. It's advice many people ignore. What if you're now in your forties and you haven't even started?

The good news is you don't have to panic. But you do have to get serious about it. Making up for lost time could mean cutting back on your spending. If you don't start saving until your forties, you'll need to set aside 20 percent of your gross income. If you wait until your fifties, your target will have to be 30 percent. As a last resort, you may have to sell your house, your cottage, and your second car; get a second job; and reduce your leisure spending. Recent changes in tax laws by Congress also help. Late starters can put double the amount away for retirement in their prime earning years—fifty and beyond—to help lessen the blow of dragging their feet and starting their retirement planning so late.

If you're lucky enough to start investing early, you can take more risk. That doesn't mean putting all your money into penny stocks. But it does mean having a greater percentage of your investments in higher-earning equities rather than the more cautious Treasury and savings bonds that many people select as they get older.

Consider these examples:

• If you start investing $100 a month at age twenty-five into a retirement account that gains 10 percent a year, by age sixty-five you'll have $632,000. But if you don't start investing the same amount until you're thirty-five, you'll only take away $226,000 when you retire. Starting at twenty-five will get you $406,000 more, at a cost of only $12,000.

- If you set aside $200 a month at a 10.2 percent return, you could start investing at age twenty-one and stop ten years later and have a $1 million nest egg at age sixty-five. That means a $22,000 investment over one decade gets you $1 million down the road. Of course, assuming continued inflation, $1 million then won't buy you what $1 million would today. But it'll buy you a heck of a lot more than nothing will.

The Rule of 72

Here's a trick some financial planners use. To find out how many years it will take your mutual fund investment to double, divide the annual rate of return by 72. So at a 7 percent return, your money will double in ten years and quadruple in twenty years. Financial gurus call it "the rule of 72."❖

Case Study: *Taking Charge*

Arden Hawes had heard it all before.

The thirty-three-year-old grade school teacher had heard from her parents, her grandparents, and her coworkers about how she had to start paying more attention to her personal finances.

"Heck, I was even starting to hear it from some of my students," she joked.

She began reading up on the topic and soon learned that she was nowhere near ready to take command of her long-term financial needs because she hadn't built any foundation to work from. "I'd read where financial experts said you need 70 to 80 percent of your preretirement income to live comfortably once you quit working," she says. "I recalled thinking that if I retired like I planned to at age fifty-five, I could still easily live into my nineties, like many members of my family have. But could I afford to?"

Arden went right to work building a computer spreadsheet detailing where she was financially, how much she was spending and how much she was bringing in, and how much she estimated she needed to live on in retirement.

"I found one of those 'retirement calculators' they have on the Web and plugged all my information in. I made sure that I included my husband's salary and the projected cost of sending my two kids to college and the projected cost of my daughter's wedding to her boyfriend Cooper. It really opened my eyes to the work that was ahead of me."

Still, Arden was glad she finally had a blueprint to work from for planning her family's financial future. "It's funny," she says. "I always took financial planning for granted. But once I found out that I was the best person available to make sure I met my financial needs, well, the rest was easy. I knew right then that I had to take control because, despite what the big brokerage and mutual fund firms say, nobody else was going to know my financial picture as well as I would."

Arden Hawes Personal Portfolio
ALLOCATION PERCENTAGES
30% long-term stable value stocks
25% large-cap growth stocks
15% mid-cap stocks
10% growth and income stocks
10% small-cap aggressive growth stocks
10% international stocks
FOLIO FAVORITES
Intel, McDonald's, Walt Disney

Chapter Checklist

✓ A personal balance sheet is your first step on the road to a successful personal portfolio; setting long-term financial goals is the next step.

✓ When you set your goals, be specific. Aim for clear targets such as "$2,000 into a retirement account," rather than generalities like "contribute to savings."

✓ A recent survey by a Big Four accounting firm shows that unless we save a great deal more than we currently do, three out of four Americans over the age of twenty will have less than half the money they need to retire to maintain their preretirement standard of living.

✓ Other good foundations from which to build your own personal portfolio: Estimate how much you'll need to retire in comfort; develop a savings plan; start saving now; and get some good life insurance.

Chapter 4

Stocking Up

*"Some people drink from the fountain
of knowledge. Others just gargle."*
—Anonymous

ou can be rich or you can be poor, but ask anyone in
the former category which is better and they'll tell
you that wealth is the way to go.

That's not to say that poverty doesn't have its advantages.
If you're mired in debt at age seventy, at least your children
won't have you declared legally insane in order to gain control of your estate. And having nothing in the bank isn't a big
problem as long as you own that rare blood type.

Too harsh? Probably. But I'm trying to make a point here.
The path to wealth is littered with do-it-yourself investors who
never made it to the promised land because they lost their focus
and forgot the mantra for financial market wealth creation:

Invest in stocks.

Investing in stocks is by far your best bet for meeting your
financial dreams. Bonds are fine, but at best they provide a
good buffer in periods when the stock market is in decline.
Most bonds are also guaranteed by Uncle Sam so the risk of losing any money you invest in them is very low.

Unfortunately, "very low" is the term Wall Street professionals often use to describe the returns you get from investing in bonds and their fixed-income counterparts, money
market investments.

Still, balance and diversification count for a lot in an investment portfolio. So, by all means, make sure you include some bonds in your personal portfolio. Perhaps the best way to do that is to invest in a bond index fund and use that as ballast for your stock-based personal portfolio. Though we'll talk more about the ratio of stocks and bonds in your investment portfolio in the chapter on asset allocation, it's usually best to beef up the bulk of your portfolio with stocks. This is especially true if you're younger and have more time to recover from the inevitable down markets that stocks can and do experience.

But to make any money in the financial markets—any real money, that is—you have to be in stocks during the more frequent times, historically, that stocks have risen in the financial markets.

Let's look at how the performance of stocks over the years bears out that statement, especially when compared to the performance of bonds and how both do versus inflation:

Performance of Stocks vs. Bonds: 1926–2000		
SECURITY TYPE	COMPOUND ANNUAL RETURN	AFTER TAXES AND INFLATION
Small Company Stocks	12.4%	5.91%
Large Company Stocks	11.2%	5.04%
Govt. Bonds	5.3%	0.75%
T-bills	3.8%	0.34%

Inflation: 3.1%

Source: Ibbotson Associates.

Although stocks have taken a beating versus bonds in the first years of the twenty-first century, stocks built up such a big advantage during the 1990s that they still come out ahead on a short-term basis:

Stocks vs. Bonds: 1990–2001 Annualized Returns
Standard & Poor's 500 Index: 12.2 percent
Lehman Brothers Bond Index: 8.4 percent

Still not convinced? Okay, think of it this way. If you were alive back in 1926 and had invested $1 in large-company stocks, left unsold, that $1 would have risen to $2,351 by December 31, 1998. But if you had invested that $1 in thirty-year government bonds in 1926, your $1 would have only grown to $44.

That's quite a compelling case for stocks, even though stocks have ticked off many an investor in recent years—investors who have seen their 401(k)'s turn into 201(k)'s, as the joke goes. Over the long haul, even through fits and starts, stocks are the best way to create wealth in your personal portfolio.

Now let's take a look at stocks and how they work.

What Is a Stock?

There was a great commercial a few years back from the discount brokerage firm Ameritrade. In the ads, ordinary Americans were treated like royalty by airline crews and restaurant concierges because they were announced as "the owner of Dell Computer" or "the owner of Nike." A nice play on words, right? In actuality, the ordinary Joes and Janes were owners of a few shares of Dell and a few shares of Nike—the result of their buying stocks through Ameritrade.

Very clever, and at least technically, very correct.

That's because whether you own a million shares in a company or just one share, you're both part owners of the business. Stocks are a bit magical that way. While we can't be like Bill Gates or Michael Dell, we can own a small piece of their companies by buying stock in them. That's the apparent beauty of stocks.

From a financial viewpoint, owning a piece of a company is a good thing, especially if the company grows and the value of the company as expressed through its stock price grows with it. On average, the value of U.S. stock grows about 12 percent a year. Who wouldn't want to be the owner of a company whose value grew by 12 percent a year? That's the real beauty of stocks—you can own a small piece of one and share in the spoils as it grows in value.

What's This "Share" Business?

A *share* of a stock is a legal document that states to the world that you are the owner of that company. While the days of keeping richly engraved shares of stock in the safe behind that painting of Whistler's mother are over, the idea remains the same. These days, chances are your shares of a company's stock are held in an account with your name on it at a brokerage firm where it's registered in your name in what the financial industry refers to as "street name." All account information is also recorded and stored (usually in a computer database) at the bank or trust company acting as the stock's "custodian" and your company's transfer agent. Sounds like a lot of paperwork, right? Actually, in the online age, it's not. Wall Street needs to be able to move stock shares around quickly. It had better in an era where one billion shares of stocks may be traded on a given day.

What Rights Do I Have as Owner of a Stock?

Besides being able to brag to your buddies at the diner about being an owner of Microsoft, owning stocks also, as the commercial says, has its privileges. As a shareholder, you can:

- Vote on candidates for your company's board of directors.
- Vote on corporate mergers that affect your company.
- Attend the annual meeting of your company's stockholders.
- Receive any dividends that your company hands out.
- Receive a copy of your company's annual report and other proxy materials for the annual meeting.

You don't really have to attend a company shareholder meeting, although the buffet is usually pretty good and, if you're lucky, there's an open bar. What most shareholders usually do is vote by "proxy" on a ballot sent by the company whose stock they own.

What's All This about "Common" and "Preferred" Stocks?

When it comes to issuing stocks, companies want to have it both ways. That's why they offer investors two types of stocks that translate into two types of investment opportunities: common stocks and preferred stocks. Common stocks are much more prevalent. Chances are these are the types of stocks you'll be including in your personal portfolio. Preferred stocks are a step up the stock issuance ladder. Let's have a look at both.

Common Stock

It's not called "common" for nothing. Common stocks are the stocks we described earlier. You know, the ones that give you the right to vote at shareholder meetings and give you direct ownership in the company. They're also the types of stocks that pay you dividends and have annual reports mailed directly to your home.

That's the good news. Unfortunately, in this man's stock issuance army, common stocks are only a buck private compared to the sergeant's status of awarded preferred stocks. (Banks, brokerages, and other institutional bigwigs make up the five-star-general portion of the outfit). Take the issuance of dividends. Yes, they are paid to owners of common stocks, but only after preferred shareholders get their money first. If a company goes bankrupt, as Enron did, the firm's bond-holders and preferred stock shareholders get paid first.

Preferred Stock

Preferred stocks also offer shareholders a measure of stability in the stock investment universe. Besides being given priorities on dividend payments, preferred stockholders also get a break on what Wall Street calls "fixed" dividends. How? Preferred stock dividends are usually awarded at a fixed rate similar to interest on a fixed-income investment like a Treasury bond or a bank CD. Yes, the rate is fixed. But companies have a loophole available to give preferred shareholders higher dividends if they want. You can't fool around with the fixed interest on bond investments, but preferred shareholder dividends are another story.

One option preferred investors don't have is the right to vote at shareholder meetings. Companies theorize that since preferred stockholders are given a break on dividend payments, they shouldn't be able to enjoy that privilege *and* the right to vote on company issues as well.

Can Anyone Buy Stock?

Basically, yes. In fact, there's a veritable smorgasbord of investors who often buy stock. Besides everyday mom-and-pop investors, you also have corporations, institutional investors (like banks and insurance companies), mutual funds, and securities broker-dealer firms. According to the New York Stock Exchange there are roughly 50 million direct stockholders in the United States today. That means about one of every five adults in the United States owns stocks.

What's a "Dividend"?

Dividends—as our discussion on common and preferred stocks attests—are a way for companies to distribute profits directly to shareholders that transcends the buy-and-sell formula found on the various stock exchanges. Dividends are a great way to reward loyal investors by giving them what pointy-headed economists call "current income." Dividend payments are usually doled out by companies in relatively stable industries like utilities or consumer goods. Efforts are underway in Congress to widen the net that companies can cast out with dividends, so more relatively volatile industries like high technology or telecommunications companies can pay dividends out to their shareholders, too.

What's a Stock "Split"?

No, it's not a milkshake you can buy on Wall Street. Stock splits are another way to reward investors, usually given out by a company after a big climb in its stock price. With a stock split, shares of company stock are divided into more shares. For example, a 2-for-1 split of 100 shares presently owned results in 200 shares for the stockholder after the split. Investors hold twice as many shares, and the price of each share is "split" to half of its former price. Investors love stock splits because they are usually a good indication that a company is performing very well, in its industry as well as in the overall stock market. A split is a way to make shares more appealing to the average investor by keeping the price per share in a "reasonable" range.

Why Do Stock Prices Fluctuate?

Stocks move up and down for a wide variety of reasons. Much of it is plain old investor emotion. Some of it is the renowned "herd" mentality you've probably heard about on Wall Street, where the many follow the supposedly knowledgeable few.

Basically, it all comes down to corporate earnings—in other words, how well a company is doing at making money. If a company hemorrhages money over a short period of time, the stock price will probably decline. Conversely, if it is swimming in profits, the price of the company's stock will rise.

What can impact earnings? Lots of things—but only three primary ones you must know about:

- **The Company Effect**—Industry market share, performance of senior management, delays in getting products out, and poor customer service are just a few examples of internal company factors that can affect earnings, and thus impact the company's stock price. Take Apple Computers, for example. The company's stock price was languishing until founder Steve Jobs was brought out of retirement to restore some much-needed juice to the computer company. Jobs brought along an infusion of new ideas, like the popular iMac computer, that restored consumers' faith in the firm. As a result, company stock rebounded upward (though not as high as when the company took off in the 1980s).
- **The Industry Effect**—In a global marketplace where information is a commodity, taking the industry lead is a big factor in the success of a company's stock. With global competition, improvements in technology, savvier consumer perceptions, and the cost of running a company all impact earnings and stock prices of companies in a given industry. Look at the telecommunications industry. When it hit critical mass in 2000 or so—meaning just about everyone had a phone or Internet hookup—there were fewer new markets to crash and, consequently, fewer places to find new sources of earnings. The dearth of market opportunities pulverized the industry. By 2003, it still had not recovered.
- **The Market Effect**—Economic conditions, political influences like war and deficits, and geopolitical issues like currency fluctuations and debt all affect the consumer markets that companies are trying to reach. Consider the U.S. economy, which for months was virtually held hostage by the struggle over whether there would be a war between the United States and Iraq in early 2003. With consumers and businesses on pins and needles, people were buying less and investing less—at least, until the war ended and the market rebounded.

What Moves the Stock Market?

It's a tale of two beasts when it comes to the stock market. On the one hand, it's strong and sturdy enough to have survived, among other things, two world wars, a depression, several recessions, and a direct attack on New York City in 2001.

On the other hand, the stock market can be a fragile beast on a day-to-day basis. From hour to hour and even minute to minute, the market is easily swayed by economic news, industry events, and political developments, among other triggers. Here's a list of the factors that are most likely to move the market in one direction or another:

Positive impact on stock markets:

- Economic expansion (Gross Domestic Product, consumer goods)
- Interest rate cuts
- Tax cuts
- Rising corporate profits
- Political stability
- High employment rate
- Loose money supply

Negative impact on stock markets:

- Recession
- Interest rate increases
- Tax increases
- Declining or stagnant corporate profits
- International conflicts and pending elections
- High unemployment rate
- Tight money supply

Source: Securities Industry Association's "SIA Investor" Web site, 2003.

Understanding Market Corrections

The stock market is a dynamic place, ebbing and flowing along on a tide of investor emotions, economic numbers, and big moves by Wall Street's heavy hitters.

Sometimes these factors—and some of the others I mentioned earlier—can move the market dramatically. If the market moves up significantly and for a sustained period, Wall Street types call that a "bull market." When it moves down significantly—10 percent is a good rule of thumb—then the experts say it's a "bear market," or what is also known as a "market correction."

Corrections are usually cyclical, and can happen on any timetable—maybe once or twice annually or maybe—like in the 1990s—only once or twice a decade. Some professional traders believe that self-correcting markets are a good thing for investors. They say that a correction recalculates stock prices at more reasonable prices after they've shot up for one reason or another.

Speculative Bubbles

U.S. investors have been "bubbled" to distraction in recent years, most notably with the dot-com bubble of the late 1990s and early 2000s. What are these bubbles and what does it mean when they pop?

A speculative bubble occurs when stock prices rise to unsustainable levels, fueled primarily by investor optimism. If you're a history buff, you catch on pretty quick that investment bubbles usually precede periods of significant market decline. Besides the dot-com bubble of the 1990s, we had the high technology bubble of 1987 and the across-the-board bubble of the late 1920s. All were followed by huge stock market crashes.

Bubbles tie in to what's known as the "herd" mentality on Wall Street. A bubble bursts when a few big names sell their stocks and others follow. Then still more follow and before you know it you have a stampede of investors in a state of frenzied "sell-mania." Historically, it takes years for markets that were victimized by bubble bursts to regain their ground. One exception to this rule was in 1987—the 500-point decline in the Dow Jones Average was regained within months.

The key is to remember that stock market bubbles can't hurt you as much if you are a buy-and-hold, or long-term, investor. By staying disciplined and resisting the urge to sell when seemingly everyone else is selling, you can ride out market declines triggered by investment bubbles.

A good rule of thumb from financier Warren Buffett: He said that in order to make money on Wall Street, "buy when others are selling and sell when others are buying."

What Are Cyclical Markets?

When you begin building your own mutual funds, you'll want to take into consideration the realities of cyclical investing. All this means is that stocks—particularly stocks in certain industries—follow predictable patterns. Such ebbs and flows are determined by a given asset class, or a given industry is impacted by economic events.

Historically, cyclical stocks do well in flush economic periods and fall back in times when the economy tanks. Hotel, travel, and retail stocks suffer when the economy is in decline, as people stop traveling and reduce their expenditures on clothing and household consumer goods. But when the good times roll again, people will resume traveling and buying blue jeans and CD players.

Some stocks seem bulletproof to cyclical market patterns. Utility, health-care, and food and beverage stocks usually defy the cyclical market theory because people buy these products in good times and in bad. Think of the old joke about the liquor industry. People drink to celebrate and they drink to drown their sorrows. Either way, they're drinking.

Where Do Investors Buy Stocks?

For your personal portfolio, you'll likely wind up buying the stocks you want through a folio firm or a discount broker. These outlets are flourishing thanks to the evolution of online trading via the Internet.

Historically, though, investors have purchased their stocks through other means, primarily through brokerage firms—or what the investment industry calls "broker-dealers."

When investors place an order to buy or sell stocks, the brokerage firm takes that money and executes the customer's order from stock held in inventory, or else the broker may go to a securities exchange to "fill" the order.

Broker-dealers charge a fee, called a commission, for buying and selling stocks for investors. Commissions usually amount to a small percentage of the stock value purchased or sold. Since commissions are charged both for buying and for selling stocks, investors are generally better off holding their stock and not selling frequently. Unless stock prices appreciate very quickly, commissions may offset any profits made over a short period of time.

Where Can I Get More Information about Buying Stocks?

These days there is no shortage of places to go to learn more about stocks. For the heavy-duty stuff, head straight to Standard & Poor's *(standardandpoors.com)*, Moody's *(moodys.com)*, Hoover's Online *(hoovers.com)*, and Value Line *(valueline.com)*. Each company has a huge inventory of information on stocks and stock trading. Also bone up on stocks by reading top-notch publications like *Forbes, Fortune, Worth*, and, of course, *The Wall Street Journal*.

For a truly objective take on stocks, visit both the Securities and Exchange Commission *(www.sec.org)* and the Securities Industry Association *(www.siainvestor.com)*.

Some Sound Strategies for Buying Stocks

Watch for these underlying factors (fundamentals) to gauge a company's profitability:

- Large market share
- Well-known product
- Sound management
- Strong history of corporate earnings

The Most Important Reason for Choosing Stocks

There are plenty of good reasons to own stocks, but perhaps the most critical one is that, over time, stocks are your best chance of earning more than the rate of inflation.

Inflation can really take a bite out of your pocketbook. It's the increase in the price of goods and services that, averaged out annually, raises the cost of living by about 3 percent per year—every year. Like rust, inflation never sleeps. That's why you need some rust protection in the form of stocks in your investment portfolio.

If your investment returns don't keep pace with inflation, your long-term financial future is in real trouble. This is the reason for taking a close look at an investment's *nominal* return (its return before inflation is taken into account) and an investment's *real* return (the rate of return after inflation has been taken into account).

Let's take a look at the difference between nominal and real returns.

The average rate of inflation: 1926–1996 = 3.3 percent

Stocks: $1 invested in U.S. large company stocks (as expressed by the Standard & Poor's 500 Index) from 1926 through 1996 would have earned 12.4 percent on an average annual return. That's the nominal return.

Nominal return = 12.4 percent
Real return = 9.1 percent

Bonds: $1 invested in T-bills over the same seventy-year time frame would have earned a 3.9 percent nominal return.

Nominal return = 3.9 percent
Real return = 0.6 percent

So, don't be fooled by Wall Street hucksters who talk only about an investment's nominal returns. Stop them in their tracks by asking about the real rate of return.

What Are the Risks of Owning Stocks?

First and foremost, the value of your stock may go down, even disappear. But that doesn't happen often, especially if you do your homework and invest in companies that make good products, have good management, and generate solid profits. Still, as part owner of a given company, you're taking more risk in actually owning the stocks than you are if you, for example, loan a company your money in the form of a bond investment. With bonds, there's a guarantee built in to your investment that you'll get your principal (the amount you invested) back, plus accrued interest. It's set in stone.

Stocks aren't like that. There's no flat-out guarantee that you'll earn any money. Heck, you can even lose it all. If the company pulls an Enron and goes bankrupt, shareholders are among the last folks to get their money back, behind the armies of bankers and lawyers and IRS agents standing in line ahead of you. If there's anything left, the shareholders can divvy up the proceeds. But by then, after the professional vultures have filled their bellies, there's usually little left on the carcass of any value.

That's the bad news. Now for the good news. Sooner or later, the stock market will notice the company you diligently researched and invested your money in. When it does—and sees the wonderful things that your company is doing—it rewards the company and its shareholders by raising the price of the stock and increasing the company's value. When a stock price goes up, that means demand for the stock is high (i.e., everybody wants in on a good thing). Since more folks want to be like you and own the same stock, the price of the stock goes up correspondingly. It's all supply and demand, folks. If you really harness your portfolio to a winner—a Disney, a Microsoft, a Wal-Mart—the return on your investment can go much higher than the 11 percent or 12 percent that stocks historically earn. Those stories about Microsoft secretaries retiring as multimillionaires aren't just urban legends. Plenty of people who bought that stock early and hung onto it saw their investments rise astronomically. But that's the payoff for taking more risk with your investments.

How Do Companies Go "Public"?

By and large, companies start off as little hatchlings, incubating for a while as private companies, growing and gathering strength for the day when (most of them) will go public and be traded on one of the big stock exchanges like the New York Stock Exchange or NASDAQ.

Companies that do decide to go public have to go through a rigorous due diligence process in which the underwriting investors—usually an investment banking firm—will kick tires and take temperatures and generally act like pests to find out how much, if anything, a company should be valued on the open stock market. When that decision is made, and ABC, Inc. is set to go public at $15 a share, the underwriters of the company stock hold what's called an initial public offering (IPO) where the stock is first offered to interested buyers in the marketplace. Usually, the fat clients and big institutional investors get first crack at an IPO—as a reward for the hefty fees and commissions they pay out to the underwriting investment banking firms. After the IPO is offered, the stock is available to anyone who wants it. There you have it: A stock is born.

> ## Americans Are Loading Up on Stocks
> According to the Washington-based Investment Company Institute, the growth in individual stock ownership rose from 30.2 million U.S. shareowners in 1980 to 84.3 million in 2002.❖

What's the Secret of Stock Ownership Success?

We'll talk more in subsequent chapters about the keys to finding good stocks. But, for a taste of what's to come, think as the Big Dogs do. Highly successful investors like Warren Buffett and Peter Lynch take a common-sense approach to picking stocks. When push comes to shove, they like to buy stock in good companies at a reasonable price. Sure, there's more to it than that, but if you keep that philosophy in mind when you invest in stocks, you'll greatly improve your chances of picking winners, again and again, as the Big Dogs do.

What Types of Stocks Are There?

Stock asset classes are like the weather in New England. If you don't like what you're getting, wait five minutes and something else will come along.

Before we sketch out some asset classes you should know about, let's take a moment and look at some of the terms we'll be seeing when we discuss asset classes in this book:

Market Capitalization
Market capitalization—or market cap for short—is the favorite method used by Wall Street types to categorize stock. Market cap is calculated by multiplying a company's current stock price by the number of its existing shares. For instance, a stock with a current market value of $20 a share

and a hundred million shares of existing stock would have a market cap of $2 billion.

Wall Street observers just love using market cap calculations to categorize stocks. Instead of attaching dollar figures to each asset class, it's easier to say that large-cap stocks are companies that have assets valued at $100 million or more.

Here's a snapshot of how Wall Street categorizes stocks via market capitalization:

- Large-cap stocks: $5 billion or more in assets.
- Mid-cap stocks: $2 billion to $5 billion in assets.
- Small-cap stocks: $1 billion to $2 billion in assets.
- Micro-cap stocks: Up to $1 billion in assets.

By and large, the larger the market capitalization, the more stable the company and its stock price. For example, Ford Motor Co., a multibillion-dollar company, is going to demonstrate more stability in its stock price than the latest bio-tech company that just went public and hasn't earned a lot of money yet.

Small-cap stocks were the darling of the investment world in the late 1990s, mostly in the form of those wicked dot-com stocks we've all heard about. Investors poured billions into questionable small-cap offerings like Furniture.com and eToys.com, only to see those companies—and thousands more like them—go belly-up.

Meanwhile, large company stocks like Ford, 3M, and Procter & Gamble saw their stocks go relatively ignored in the rush to find the next eBay or Amazon.com. But the large-cap stocks had the last laugh in the early 2000s as their stock prices held much steadier than small-cap stocks did (although bonds outperformed both sectors from 2000 to 2003).

The trouble with small-cap stocks is that these companies are usually much younger and don't have the deep pockets to weather tough economic storms like the big boys do. Mid-cap stocks proved an oasis of sorts for investors during those troubled years. Like Goldilocks and her porridge, they proved not too hot and not too cold for millions of anxious investors. Think Harley-Davidson, Outback Steakhouse, and Pitney Bowes.

Types of Stocks

There are as many types of stocks as there ice cream flavors at Baskin-Robbins. The primary ones you'll need to know about are as follows:

- **Blue-chip stocks**—These are the oldest and historically most profitable companies. The vast majority of the thirty Dow stocks are blue-chippers. These are the stocks that Wall Street traders consider as having the lowest risk for stock investors. They're also the most likely stock to pay a dividend. Think IBM and General Electric as good examples of blue-chip stocks.

- **Growth stocks**—These are stocks that the experts consider to have the best potential for solid earnings. They usually don't pay dividends because they reinvest their earnings for growth. Known as stocks with a tremendous "upside," growth stocks get their name because they have the highest potential for growth of any asset class. What goes up quickly can go down quickly as well. Growth stocks can plummet far and fast given bad financial or economic news. Think of Microsoft, Dell, Intel, and eBay as growth stocks.

- **Income stocks**—Income stocks are stocks that regularly pay dividends. These are typically entrenched companies with substantial earnings. The stock prices of such stocks usually move glacially over longer time periods.

In Chapters 6 and 7, we'll take a closer look at stocks and stock asset classes.

What Are Stock Options?

My first job on Wall Street was as a "runner" on the Philadelphia Stock Exchange's equity options floor. As a brash twenty-two-year-old, I felt my lack of knowledge of stock options would be easily surmountable and that I'd be trading them on my own in no time.

Well, eighteen years later, I'm still not trading options. They're extremely sophisticated, wildly volatile, and possess the ability to turn you from a prince into a pauper in an afternoon's worth of trading.

But far be it from me to tell you to stay away from trading stock options in your personal portfolio (even though that's precisely what you should do). But if you prove immune to such good advice, here's a brief primer on stock options.

Basically, stock options are an investment tool that enables one to benefit from a movement in a stock's price without directly buying the stock. Investors buy what is known as a "call" option if they believe a stock is going to go up. Conversely, an investor buys what is known as a "put" option if they think a stock is about to decline in price.

Buying a stock option gives one the right, but not the obligation, to buy or sell a specified amount of stock (typically traded in 100-share "lots") at a specified price (called the strike price) during a specified period of time (up until the expiration date).

Here's an example. If the date is August 10 and XYZ Co. is trading at $50 a share, an investor could buy a September $55 call option for $1.50. The actual cost of the option is $150 because it is for 100 shares, so one multiplies 1.50 times 100 shares. Options expire on the third Friday of the month. As the stock moves up and down, the value of the option will go up and down. Option investors do not have to wait until the expiration date to make money buying or selling options. They are sold throughout the entire day and the price fluctuates throughout the day based on the movement of the stock. An investor can buy one or more options depending on how much stock he or she had planned on originally purchasing.

Options are highly leveraged—and highly risky—investments. Investors are only required to invest about 10 percent of what would be required to invest in the stock directly to get the same dollar return. That leverage can severely penalize you if the stock plummets. You can lose all of your investment if the stock moves against you and you fail to sell before the expiration date.

If you are not very clear how options work (and even if you are), you should get your broker's help on your first few trades.

For more information on investing in stock options, the Chicago Board of Trade—the largest stock option trading exchange in the world—has loads of information on its Web site. Check it out at *www.cboe.org*.

Stock Options Aren't Dead Yet

According to the firm Hewitt & Associates, companies are still fairly bullish on handing out stock options as a reward incentive for employees and as a less-expensive option than handing out raises. According to Hewitt, 80 percent of surveyed organizations currently have some form of employee stock ownership programs (ESOPs), usually in the guise of variable pay plans. In 1995 that figure was only 59 percent. ❖

Investing Overseas: Have Portfolio, Will Travel

Stock ownership is hardly limited to the listings on the New York Stock Exchange or on the NASDAQ. In fact, stocks are traded around the clock, and around the world on exchange floors and electronic markets. Markets in London open before those in Singapore close, and London is still open when trading begins in New York.

That's a situation you may want to take advantage of, as international stocks can be a welcome addition to your personal portfolio. International stocks not only give your portfolio a wider diversification benefit, they also enable you to take advantage of growth opportunities in other economies.

You may not have heard the news, but international investments outperformed U.S. investments over large portions of the past thirty-five years or so, as defined by the Standard & Poor's 500 (S&P 500) Index and Morgan Stanley Capital International Europe, Australasia, Far East (MSCI/EAFE) Index. For much of the latter half of the twentieth century, overseas stock investing was a well-kept secret.

Not anymore. International investing is a big deal these days, mostly for its profit potential and its diversification benefits. Overseas diversification works much like sector and industry stock market allocations work (there's much more on this topic in Chapter 5). When the stock market in one country is struggling, the comparable market in another country could be on the rise. Rising prices in developed European markets, or in markets such as Thailand, for example, sometimes outpace growth in the United States. Of course, sending your portfolio dollars to countries you've never set foot in presents some risk challenges of its own. You could be exposing yourself to risks of currency, economic, or political instability that you may not face with a U.S.–only personal portfolio.

Plus, if you buy your international stocks directly from a foreign bourse, like the Tokyo Stock Exchange or the Bangkok Stock Exchange, you might experience some problems.

Clearing of trades could be slower, and there may be questions about who has custody of your securities. Plus, your buy and sell orders may be complicated by language and timing barriers, even if you trade online. What's more, fluctuations in currency values and currency exchange fees may eat into profits. Lastly, taxes on gains and losses may be handled differently than in the United States.

Case Study: *In It for the Long Haul*

"When I began looking into taking control over my own investments, I was still on the fence, so to speak, about balancing my portfolio equally between stocks, bonds, and cash," says Mary Ellen Nostrand, a thirty-four-year-old soccer mom and do-it-yourself investor. "Up until that point our family investment portfolio was one-third stocks, one-third bonds, and one-third cash. My husband didn't mind but, after doing some research on the benefits of stocks and how they compound over time, I really felt like we were missing out by not being a bit more aggressive."

Locking the kids out of the home office, Mary Ellen logged onto the Web and began scouring sites like CBS News Marketwatch and *The Wall Street Journal's WSJ.com* for as much information on stocks as she could find. "I realized that there is some higher risk with stocks, but I felt the data indicated that the risk/reward ratio was in favor of stocks—not against them."

She felt history backed that assessment up fairly easily. "If you look back in history, at the generation that began investing in 1940, you see that their level of wealth came from investing in stocks over the long run. It seems so obvious but I don't think people, including many of my friends, realize that.

"Or, if they do, they don't think about the long haul."

Mary Ellen Nostrand Personal Portfolio
ALLOCATION PERCENTAGES
20% value stocks
15% equity income stocks
15% international stocks
20% growth stocks
30% municipal bonds
FOLIO FAVORITES
Delta Airlines, UPS, Dell Computer

Chapter Checklist

✓ Stocks give you direct ownership in a company. With bonds, you're only lending the company money with the understanding that it will be paid back in full, plus interest.

On the other hand, there is no guarantee you'll recoup any money lost investing in stocks.

✓ Stocks are easily the best performing investments over the long haul.

✓ Stocks are also your best investment weapon for fighting inflation, which can take a 3 or 4 percent bite out of your personal portfolio every year.

✓ A good understanding of market corrections, speculative bubbles, and cyclical investment periods can give you a leg up when building your personal portfolio.

✓ Wall Street analysts use market capitalization to measure the growth and value of a given company.

✓ Stock options are high-risk investments. Leave them to the high rollers.

✓ A great way to discover more high-growth companies—and provide some diversity to your personal portfolio—is to invest overseas.

## Chapter 5

Risk and Diversification

*"Whenever I make a bum decision,
I just go out and make another one."*
—HARRY TRUMAN

L et's spend some time talking about decisions—specifically the decisions you make that will steer your mutual fund building process.

These decisions—how much risk to take, what kind of stocks to have, how much to diversify—are the lifeblood of any investment portfolio program.

Decisions are critical. Consider Dwight D. Eisenhower in early June 1944. With D-day fast approaching, Ike had to decide exactly when to pull the trigger and attack. Finally, he said "No matter what the weather looks like, we have to go ahead now. Waiting any longer could be even more dangerous."

While our investment decisions pale in comparison to the one General Eisenhower made that week in June 1944, there's a good lesson for us in his line of thinking. There comes a point when you have to decide, one way or another, what to do. Then you do it.

It's the same with your personal portfolio, where the most important decision you'll make isn't whether you got in on that up-and-coming biotechnology company or you caught the hot emerging market sector on the way up. No, the big decisions come much earlier than that—specifically when you're calculating the makeup of your fund.

The Risk Factor

Before I get into the issue of investment risk and what it means to your portfolio, allow me to relate a story on why it's so important to know your risk tolerance and to have a good investment plan in place before you start picking stocks.

The late, great financier Jay Gould was known by the media as "The Devil of Wall Street" for his wily—and some would say conniving—ways of being on the right side of a stock at the right time. One Sunday, Gould found himself greeting his minister after church. After exchanging pleasantries, the minister mentioned that the church had recently received $20,000 in donations and asked Gould whether he had any hot tips on the market. "Sure," Gould reportedly said. "Invest the money in Missouri Pacific." Sure enough, the minister did just that. Happily, he watched the stock rise for several weeks. Unhappily, he watched it crash soon after. The crestfallen minister mentioned the bad news to Gould. Lickety-split, Gould wrote a check for the full $20,000 right on the spot. Relieved, but anxious, the minister added that he'd given the tip to many members of his congregation. "No problem," Gould answered. "They were the ones I was after all along."

While the minister lucked out in the long run, he learned a painful lesson on the importance of investment risk. Always know going in what you can afford to lose and, going forward, manage your portfolio correspondingly.

What Is Risk?

What is risk? When it comes to investing your money, it's critical. If establishing goals and having a plan is the foundation for your portfolio plan, then risk, along with diversification, is the framework. While risk is based primarily on your comfort level, it's also based on your ever-changing financial picture, your need for cash, your investment preferences, your time horizon, and other factors. Knowing your risk tolerance level is a critical factor if you're to build a dynamite personal port-folio, as it helps determine what kinds of investments best accommodate your investment goals.

That said, risk can mean different things to different people. At the high end, fooling around with risk can lead to economic disaster. That's what investors of Enron and WorldCom, just to name a few scandal-plagued companies in recent years, found out when company officials played fast and loose with billions of dollars of shareholder money. At the smaller end of the spectrum, investors in Enron and WorldCom who parked too much company stock into their portfolios—without diversifying into broader, safer investment venues—paid a whale of a price when those stocks went into freefall.

Economists—you know, those pompous windbags who are never around six months after they said the market would rise 500 points when it actually sank like an anchor—define risk as the volatility or variance in return that is created by market volatility. In plain English, what they're saying is that your stocks will, given time, move up and down. It's the "up -and-down" part that really concerns those of us who build our own mutual funds.

You see, volatility—the up-and-down thing—can wreak havoc on your portfolio's performance, cause you untold hours of lost sleep, and turn your usual sunny disposition dour, to the point where Jack the Ripper would give you a wide berth if he saw you walking down the street.

Historically, here's what you can expect to earn from the major investment asset classes on an annual basis:

Cash and money market instruments—Up to 3 percent
Real estate—Up to 5 percent
Bonds—Up to 8 percent
Stocks—Up to 12 percent

The key to understanding and managing a portfolio in an often-volatile market climate is to understand the first tenet of investment risk: You can lose money.

Let's repeat that. *You can lose money.*

That's because, unlike your savings account at the bank, your stock portfolio is not insured by the federal government against market losses. Same thing with mutual funds—they're not covered by Uncle Sam, either. The key to mitigating risk is to understand that there are various types and levels of investment risk. The common denominator is to consider the possible risk and reward and decide what works best for you.

Here's a snapshot of the different levels of risk:

- **Inflation risk**—The risk that the value of an investment will be eroded as inflation rates rise. Note that inflation, which rises about 3 percent annually, will cut about 3 percent off the value of your investment gains each year. To combat inflation risk, the idea is to invest a bit more aggressively to compensate for the bite that inflation will take out of your investment portfolio.

- **Market risk**—The risk that actions in financial markets may lead to losses in the value of your investment. Think of market risk like the three-point shot in basketball. It's farther away, but if you make the shot, then you earn more points than with a dunk or a lay-up. Of course, the odds are longer that you'll hit the three-pointer than you would the dunk or the lay-up. Translated into Wall Street lingo, market risk means that investments with a greater chance of losing value are also the investments that can generate higher returns.

- **Interest-rate risk**—The risk that the value of your investment will decline as interest rates rise. That's especially true of bond investments. When rates rise, the value of your bond portfolio declines. When rates decline, the value of your bond portfolio increases. We'll talk more about investment diversification later in this chapter, but one way to offset the impact of interest-rate risk is to have a healthy share of stocks in your portfolio (heck—you would anyway) and dilute the potential impact of interest-rate risk.

• **Credit risk**—The risk that an obligation will not be paid. Again, more of an issue for bond investors, particularly in the high-yield (more informally known as "junk" bond) category. In the bond world, the higher the yield, the more risk you're taking. (Think about it: Why would a company offer you a higher return if it didn't have to? Answer: It has to— because otherwise smart investors would stay away.) But with higher risk comes the possibility of default. Think of credit risk as a loan to a college buddy. You knew the risk of not being paid back is real. Naturally, the deadbeat blows you off and never pays you back. That's the downside of credit risk.

• **Diversification risk**—The risk that if you put all your eggs in one basket—as many Enron investors did—your financial fortunes are tied to the financial fortunes of that lone company. Big mistake, as the Enron shareholders discovered. After all, why bet on just one horse when you can bet on as many as you want?

• **Liquidity risk**—The risk that an investor will not be able to buy or sell an investment quickly because buying and selling opportunities are limited. Obviously, not every stock is in high demand. If you buy a stock in a company that begins acting like a young Jerry Lewis, with the flailing and the yelling and the hysteria and the "Oys!" and "Uh-oh's," you may have a difficult time selling it, even though you may need the cash. That's liquidity risk.

• **Currency risk**—The risk that an investment transacted in a foreign currency will lose value due to fluctuations in the rate of exchange. That's the trouble with foreign investments. Your money gets to go to places you've never been. Worse, it stays there if the country in question experiences some economic troubles. The good news is that no self-respecting foreign bourse *wants* you to think your money may pull a fast one and never come back. So political and business leaders pull out all the stops to minimize the chance of any currency risk. In certain hot spots, like the Middle East or Eastern Europe, the chance of currency risk is higher than in more sedate locales like the Pacific Rim or Western Europe. Of course, there are no guarantees. Some Wall Street types also refer to currency risk as "political risk." Same idea, but directed more to the threat of political instability than economic instability (as if, these days, the two could be separated).

• **"Status quo" risk**—The risk of doing nothing is perhaps your greatest risk of all. Standing idly by and allowing your portfolio to twist slowly in the wind because you don't want to take on *any* risk is a surefire portfolio killer. You've got to take on some risk if you're going to make any money on your investments. So remember, status quo kills.

A Word on Volatility

Funny thing about stocks. Like your Uncle Fred after a few too many beers at the family holiday picnic, stocks are all over the place. These ups and downs are known to professional traders as volatility.

Some investments are more susceptible to volatility than others. Stocks, for example, swing much more wildly than do bonds. But even within the stock sector, volatility varies. Blue-chip companies, which have been around longer and are more stable, are less likely to be as volatile as stocks in smaller or newer companies.

Interesting note: Sure, volatility can have you reaching for the Pepto-Bismol. But if you can ride out the short-term gyrations, chances are you'll gain more over the long haul. That's because stocks, the most volatile of all financial vehicles, offer the greatest returns. ❖

What's Your Risk Tolerance?

Are you a worrywart? Do you tremble with anxiety at the thought of ordering the "DefCon 5" buffalo wings, opting instead for the milder version? Do you wear sensible shoes, opt for the rust coating on your new car, or carry a baseball bat when you have to go to the bathroom in the middle of the night?

If so, that's okay. It just means you're the cautious type. And cautious types shouldn't load up their personal portfolios with high-risk investments.

Conversely, are you more the daredevil type? Have you ever bungee-jumped? Ridden the roller coaster at Six Flags? Brazenly dunked chocolate into your peanut butter? If so, you may have a higher tolerance for riskier investments.

But which one are you? Or are you, like most investors, somewhere in the middle? If you're not sure, what you need to do is to conduct your very own risk tolerance exam.

We'll do that in a moment, but first remember this: Like noses and navels, risk tolerance varies from person to person. Heck, even your own risk tolerance will likely change over time, as you get married, have children, buy a new home, and encounter new lifetime and economic circumstances.

Again, it goes back to what we discussed in Chapter 3—namely, goals. Is financial safety preferable to being aggressive, and all the potentially stomach-churning investment vehicles that accompany such a strategy? Can you stomach (there's that word again) losses in the short term if it means a higher chance of bigger gains over the long haul?

Basically, what risk and reward boil down to is what kind of portfolio to build that will allow you to sleep comfortably at night. If you build an aggressive portfolio full of technology stocks, emerging market stocks, and other higher-risk/higher-return investments, will it keep you up at night to the point where you're on a first-name basis with the overnight shift at the Quickie Mart? Or do you slumber peacefully at night, knowing you worked hard and found the right mix of stocks and bonds for your personal portfolio? The latter is what we're shooting for here.

Consequently, whether you consider your investment profile to be conservative, moderate, or aggressive, the goal is to figure out how anxious (or calm) you will be when your personal portfolio begins acting like a Mexican jumping bean. A tip: Ask yourself this question: How much money could I lose in a given year and still confidently stick with my investment plan? Is it 5 percent? 10 percent? 20 percent? (Hello, gastroenterologist!) Find a number you feel you can afford to lose and build your personal portfolio accordingly. As you do, remember that assuming a tad more risk also ups your odds for greater investment returns.

The Importance of Market Risk

Market risk is an important criterion in determining the makeup of your personal portfolio. Take a look for yourself:

Market Risk 1990–1999

	BEST ANNUAL RETURN	WORST ANNUAL RETURN
Stocks	+37.4%	-3.2%
Bonds	+26.3%	-7.3%
Money Markets	+8.1%	+3.2%

Now, look at the investment risk scenario from 1973 to 1999. It paints a much more volatile picture.

Market Risk 1973–1999

	BEST ANNUAL RETURN	WORST ANNUAL RETURN
Stocks	+37.4%	-26.5%
Bonds	+42.3%	-7.3%
Money Markets	+15.3%	+3.2%

Assessing Your Risk Tolerance: A Test

Trying to pin down your tolerance for risk is akin to chasing ghosts: It's an uncertain process that's forever susceptible to second-guessing. In fact, you can never be quite sure what your tolerance for risk will be from year to year. Answer these questions to find your best assessment of your risk tolerance:

1. Do market fluctuations keep you awake at night?
2. Are you unfamiliar with investing?
3. Do you consider yourself more a saver rather than an investor?
4. Does the fear of losing 50 percent of your portfolio frighten you?

If you answered "yes" to these questions, you are likely to be a "conservative" investor.

1. Are you calm even though markets may seem volatile?
2. Are you knowledgeable about investing and the securities markets?
3. Are you investing for a long-term goal?
4. Can you withstand considerable short-term losses?

If you answered "yes" to these questions, you may be a more aggressive investor.

Stocks Earn Higher Returns

Historically, the long-term return from stocks is roughly 11 percent annually. Bonds—which are less risky—have returned only about 7 percent. ❖

Know Your Economic Indicators

Some investors are under the mistaken impression that they have no business boning up on financial indicators; that these fall into the domain of nerdy economists buried in spreadsheets, charts, and graphs.

Not so. An investor who doesn't understand economic indicators is like a tourist trying to navigate a foreign country without a map. Sooner or later, you'll get lost and it might take you a while to find your way again.

Consequently, it makes sense for investors in the stock market to have a thorough understanding of how the economy works and how economic activity is measured. Here's a breakdown of the key indicators investors should know about.

Business Inventories

A monthly running total of how well companies are selling their products, business inventories are a neon signal to economists and investors alike. The business inventory data are collected from three sources: manufacturers, merchant wholesalers, and retail reports. Retail inventories are the most volatile component of inventories and can cause major swings. A sudden fall in inventories may show the onset of expansion and a sudden accumulation of inventories may signify falling demand and hence the onset of recession.

Gross Domestic Product

The gross domestic product (GDP) is the most important economic indicator published. Providing the broadest measure of economic activity, the GDP is considered the nation's report card. The four major components of the GDP are consumption, investment, government purchases, and net exports. As the barometer of the nation's total output of goods and services, GDP is the broadest of the nation's economic measures.

Consumer Price Index (CPI)

The consumer price index (CPI) is considered the most important measure of inflation. It compares prices for a fixed list of goods and services to a base period.

Unlike other measures of inflation, which only cover domestically produced goods, the CPI covers imported goods, which are becoming increasingly important to the U.S. economy.

Job Growth

Aside from the GDP, the government's employment report is the most significant economic indicator reported, setting the tone for the entire month and providing information on employment, the average workweek, hourly earnings, and the unemployment rate.

Economists use payroll jobs data to predict other economic indicators. For example, there is a strong correlation between construction payroll figures and housing starts, manufacturing and industrial production activity, total payroll and personal income. The data is also used to refine GDP estimates.

Consumers feel more at ease when the job market is expanding. But when job growth contracts to 100,000 or fewer month to month, watch out—the economy could be headed for a slowdown.

Consumer Confidence

The Conference Board maintains this index of consumer sentiment based on monthly interviews with 5,000 households. After recently hitting historical highs, the index has been falling, especially after the terrorist attacks of September 11, 2001.

In bad times or good, consumer confidence serves as a reflection of the nation's financial health. Sometimes consumers worry about inflation more than unemployment, and at other times the reverse is true. Consumer confidence is far more important to the financial markets during times of national crisis or panic, such as after the 1987 stock market crash, before and during the 1991 Persian Gulf War, after oil shocks, during recessions, and so forth.

As might be expected, consumer confidence is the weakest during recessions, slightly better on average during recoveries, and highest during expansions.

Unemployment Index

The government's employment report covers information on payroll jobs, including employment, average workweek, hourly earnings, and unemployment. Unlike the jobs data, which is a *coincident* indicator of economic activity (meaning that it changes direction at the same time as the economy), the unemployment rate is a *lagging* indicator. It increases or falls following a change in economic activity. Consequently, it is of far less significance to economists and investors.

In its favor and unlike the payroll jobs data, the unemployment rate is not subject to change. The unemployment rate has recently been running at levels below what economists believe to be the "natural rate"—that is to say, the rate at which sustained unemployment can exist without rekindling inflation. The natural rate has been pegged at 5.5 percent. Consequently, several months at levels as low as 5 percent (or lower) would have many investors and economists concerned that inflation is just around the corner.

Housing Starts

This indicator tracks how many new single-family homes or buildings were constructed throughout the month. For the survey, each house or each single apartment is counted as one housing start. (A building with 200 apartments would be counted as 200 housing starts.) The figures include all privately and publicly owned units, with the only exception being mobile homes, which are not counted.

Most of the housing start data is collected through applications and permits for building homes. The housing start data is offered in an unadjusted and a seasonally adjusted format.

According to the U.S. Census, the housing industry represents over 25 percent of investment dollars and a 5 percent value of the overall economy. Declining housing starts show a slowing economy, while increases in housing activity can pull an economy out of a downturn.

Index of Leading Economic Indicators

The index of leading economic indicators (LEI) is intended to predict future economic activity. Typically, three consecutive monthly LEI changes in the same direction suggest a turning point in the economy. For example, consecutive negative readings would indicate a possible recession.

Producer Price Index

The Producer Price Index (PPI) is a basket of various indexes covering a wide range of areas affecting domestic producers. The PPI includes industries such as goods manufacturing, fishing, agriculture, and other commodities. Each month approximately 100,000 prices are collected from 30,000 production and manufacturing firms. Three primary areas make up the PPI: industry-based, commodity-based, and stage-of-processing goods.

Other good barometers of economic growth include retail sales, employee cost index, factory purchase orders, and new and existing home sales.

The Risks of Investing in Folios

Folios are no different than mutual funds in that you can lose money by investing in them. Since personal portfolios contain securities (stocks) that rise and fall in value, the value of your personal portfolio will also rise and fall correspondingly.

You can lose money even if you build a well-diversified stock folio. While diversification lessens the severity of overall losses that may result if you hold only one stock or one type of stock, diversification doesn't protect you against all losses. When the stock market suffers widespread declines, even well-diversified folios are likely to fall in value.

It's also important to note that, unless you decide to have a financial advisor or a folio company pick your stocks, you are the one choosing the stocks for your personal portfolio. Folio firms like FOLIO*fn* will not guarantee any returns for you, even if the company winds up selecting stocks for your account. Folio companies will also not recommend any stocks to you, nor will they review your financial situation or tolerance for risk. You, and you alone, determine your risk outlook.

Note, too, that investing online and buying your stocks through the Internet, as all folio companies are set up to do, has some thorny issues as well. If a computer server crashes and you can't sell that 100 shares of Amalgamated Aardvark, the folio company you work with will not guarantee the safe execution of your trade. Or, if your computer goes on the blink, or your Internet Service Provider goes super freaky and shuts down, you're out of luck. Of course, that goes the same for anyone investing online.

What's Your Tolerance for Risk?

How much risk you can take depends on many factors: your age, your financial needs, your comfort level, how many dependents you have. If you're twenty-five years old, single, childless, and debt-free, you obviously have way more tolerance for risk than a fifty-five-year-old person with two kids in college who is nearing retirement.

The Fine Art of Diversification

Like the siphonophore, you should cover all your bases when building your own mutual fund.

Huh?

In case you didn't know, the siphonophore is a deep-sea–dwelling creature that can grow as long as a blue whale—about 130 feet long. But that's not what interests us here. For our purposes, it's instructive to note that the siphonophore can have more than a hundred stomachs (or "polyps" for you scientists out there). That means if one stomach malfunctions, there are ninety-nine others to take its place. Or if fifty somehow screw up, there are fifty more to provide backup.

Okay, I'm no marine biologist, but *that* is what I call spreading the risk. And spreading the risk is something you have to do when building your own mutual fund. And the best way to spread risk in an investment portfolio is by diversifying the types of investments you own in your portfolio.

By diversifying your investments, you're taking away the risk that one investment that's gone sour will poison the rest of your portfolio. As mentioned earlier, that's exactly what happened to the poor Enron shareholders. Most Enron employees opted to bulk up the vast majority of their 401(k) plans with company stock—a stock that ultimately proved worthless when the company declared bankruptcy in 2001.

If Enron shareholders had played it safe, and balanced out their portfolios with some nice, sage government bonds and some more predictably behaved blue-chip stocks like General Motors or Procter & Gamble, then they most likely wouldn't have suffered such a horrible fate.

But it's tough to tell someone to diversify when the one stock they have keeps going up, as in the case of pre-2001 Enron. In some cases, investors get away with it. Look at Microsoft. For years "Microsofties" loaded up their investment portfolios with company stocks, with the company's blessing (from an accounting standpoint since company stock is much cheaper for companies to give away than pay raises and bonuses). What happened? Well, truth be told, many Microsoft employees, including secretaries and other clerical workers, became millionaires.

But the chances of that happening are rare, indeed. By the early 2000s, Microsoft's stock had declined precipitously, ensuring that employees would look elsewhere to augment their investment portfolios. Sure, having some company stock is a great idea (I wish I could get my hands on some Microsoft stock on the cheap, as the firm's employees can) but, by and large, there are very few "lightning in a bottle" success stories like Microsoft in the 1980s and 1990s, or Oracle in the late 1990s. There's more of a chance that a company will go out of business than it will make you a millionaire by overloading your portfolio with its stock.

That's where diversification comes in.

Diversification simply means spreading your investments around so that all your eggs aren't in the one proverbial basket. Diversification is a real volatility killer, enabling you to cancel out much of the unnecessary risk you absorb by taking a vertical, rather than a horizontal, investment approach.

When you begin to look at the issue of diversification, one fact becomes clear: By using the strategy, you've begun to look at your portfolio as a whole, rather than as a series of disparate investments shoehorned into your portfolio like your extended family at your dining room table on Thanksgiving Day. This is a good thing.

Why? Because looking at your mutual fund as a whole is what you should do when you're making investment decisions. Yes, it could be tough to pass up Cisco or Gateway if stock prices in these companies appear reasonable. But what if you already have the tech sector covered with holdings in Dell, Compaq, and AT&T?

With diversification, you can still have the Cisco or Gateways (if you really want them) by adding them to your portfolio and taking another tech sector company, like Dell or AT&T, out of your portfolio. That way you won't get hammered if the tech sector goes into a death spiral, bringing technology stocks down with it.

The Diversification Story

All market asset classes don't respond to market events in the same way.

Portfolio #	Asset Allocation	Average Annual Return	Volatility
1.	80% Stocks; 20% Cash	21.1%	11.1%
2.	60% Stocks; 20% Bonds; 20% Cash	17.6%	8.5%
3.	40% Stocks; 40% Bonds; 20% Cash	14.1%	6.1%

Diversification Comes in Several Categories

There are several different forms of investment diversification. Let's look at the most important ones when building your own personal portfolio:

Company diversification: Here's that Enron effect again. Company diversification means spreading stocks around your portfolio so that the companies you're buying into aren't all engaged in the same business or industry. For instance, you wouldn't want to put, say, three retail manufacturing companies like The Gap, Laura Ashley, and Sears & Roebuck into your fund when one or two may do just fine. If the retail industry takes a dive, you want to absorb the impact by stocking your portfolio with stocks from other industries, like utilities or consumer goods. By ensuring you're not exposed to one particular sector, you reduce the risk to your entire personal portfolio.

Geographical diversification: It's the "one industry" effect that we just discussed, transplanted into geographical tones. Instead of loading up on all Western European, or all Latin American, or all Southeast Asian companies, why not spread the wealth and diversify across all three international sectors? That's the idea behind geographic diversification.

Asset class diversification: Same idea. You don't want to bulk up on one asset class, like large-cap stocks, or all small company stocks. You want to reduce risk and minimize volatility by diversifying among many different asset classes.

Time diversification: Some "know it alls" try to time the market and jump in when prices are low and jump back out when prices are high. But guessing when the perfect time to jump is no mean trick. After all, if predicting the direction of the stock market were easy, every Tom, Dick, and Harry would be a millionaire. Heck, ask any trader on Wall Street if they can time the market. They'll tell you they can't. Instead of relying on a Ouija board or a crystal ball to figure out where the market is going, just invest regularly. That way you're always in the market at the right time.

A Diversification Strategy

Overall, your mutual fund should be diversified into prime asset classes such as stocks, bonds, and money market investments. Additionally, you should be diversifying within those categories. In the stock portion of your own mutual fund, you should have a blend of large-, mid-, and small-cap companies. A few of those stocks should lean toward growth, others toward value.

The bond portion of your fund should be diversified, too. Bonds, money market mutual funds, and certificates of deposit are all attractive candidates for your portfolio. Cash is different. Try putting that aside in an interest-bearing account or in a money market fund at your local bank.

Here are some other diversification tips:

- Start your own mutual fund with twenty or thirty stocks from across a wide array of industries.
- Make sure you have a foreign element to your port-folio.

- Stay disciplined about asset classes: spread your money around several classes.

Not sure about the ratio of stocks to bonds? One rule is to subtract your age from 100 and keep the remainder in stocks. For example, if you're forty-five, you can safely have 55 percent of your portfolio in stocks. Don't take it literally; it's okay to cheat a bit (I do) and go to 60 percent or so.

The Different Types of Asset Classes

If you're going to dance to the diversification music adeptly, you first have to know and recognize the various kinds of asset classes there are to consider. Let's do that right now.

How many ways can you diversify your portfolio?

The Main Asset Classes

- Equity
- Global and international
- Income

The Main Stock Categories

- Large-caps (major companies with very large market capitalization)
- Mid caps and small caps (companies in which the total value of marketable shares is significantly lower than large caps)
- International and emerging market stocks

The Main Bond Categories

- Taxable and nontaxable
- Corporate-issued and government-issued
- Investment grade ("high quality") and high yield ("junk bonds")

Growth versus Value Stocks

When you begin selecting the stocks that will comprise your personal portfolio, you'll run into the terms "growth" and "value" quite a bit. Here's what you need to know.

Growth stocks are the stocks of those companies whose sales and profits are expected to grow quickly. Stock analysts are largely responsible for providing growth forecasts to the investing community. Growth stocks tend to reinvest any profits into further growth of market share or product development. As a result of this plowing-back effect, growth stocks seldom pay dividends. Instead, investors expect to earn a profit on a substantial rise in the share price.

Value stocks are the stocks of companies whose fundamental valuations are considered relatively cheap by such yardsticks of value as price-to-earnings ratios and book values.

Overall, growth stocks are a higher risk than value stocks, primarily because they're usually smaller, less-established companies without the relatively predictable earnings of value companies.

You'll also run into the term "income" stocks. These are the stocks of established companies with a history of earnings and dividend growth. Income stocks earn their name because they have a history of paying dividends. Income stocks often have the highest dividend yields available to investors. These often include the stocks of large-cap stocks and the securities of utilities. Because they generate income on a fairly predictable basis, income stocks are considered less risky than growth stocks.

Case Study: *Giving Yourself Enough Options*

Dan Bradley had just taken up golf and wasn't making much progress. That was until a friend of his pointed out that he only had five or six golf clubs in his bag while most golfers carried twelve, thirteen, or even fourteen clubs.

"He told me that I was increasing the risk of hitting the wrong shot because I didn't have enough options in my bag. For a shot that required a six-iron, for example, I was hitting a five- or even a three-iron. Naturally, my game suffered as a result."

Dan took that lesson into his personal portfolio program. When he opened his folio account, Bradley was content to stock it with five or so stocks, mostly big-name companies like IBM or Dell and leave it at that. "But the golf analogy really got me thinking. Why not decrease my chances of a major blunder by expanding the number of stocks I had in my portfolio?"

That he did, by adding a few value stocks and some growth stocks to balance out the large-cap portion of his portfolio. "I even threw in some ten-year Treasury bonds to provide safety," he adds.

Now, Bradley is thinking long term and can spend more time on his golf game since his portfolio is more diversified, and consequently, more secure.

"Now, if I could just learn to hit that new five-iron I bought."

Dan Bradley Personal Portfolio
ALLOCATION PERCENTAGES
40% small-cap growth stocks
20% mid-cap growth stocks
10% large company stocks
30% international stocks
FOLIO FAVORITES
Bank of America, Barclays, China Mobil Hong Kong

Chapter Checklist

✓ The most important decision you'll make before you start creating your personal portfolio isn't what particular stocks you'll buy. Instead, the key elements are knowing your risk level and being able to diversify your portfolio.

✓ A stock investing rule of thumb: the higher the reward potential, the higher the risk.

✓ Inflation risk, market risk, and interest rate risk are among the most prominent risk categories.

✓ What you want from your own personal portfolio is a portfolio that allows you to sleep comfortably at night.

✓ Diversity is a good way to get more restful nights. By spreading your stocks around and avoiding keeping them in just one or two stocks (as the Enron investors did), you stand a much better chance of weathering the bad times that will keep you awake.

Chapter 6

What Should Your Personal Mutual Fund Look Like?

"I'll have what she's having."
—FROM *WHEN HARRY MET SALLY*

O nce you've evaluated your risk tolerance level and promised to stay away from those Portuguese debentures, and you've latched yourself to the idea of diversification like a barnacle to the hull of a boat, it's time to figure out what your mutual fund should look like.

That's where asset allocation comes in. On Wall Street, the cognoscenti rarely agree on anything—even what to order for lunch (I know—I worked there).

But one thing most investment professionals do agree on is asset allocation. (And, no, asset allocation is not where you park your posterior throughout your house during the day.)

In Wall Street terms, asset allocation is more like investment diversification on steroids. One wag compares asset allocation to earning two quarters and then putting the coins not only in different pockets, but in different pants. That's as good a definition as any.

In more formal terms, asset allocation means investing across a variety of asset classes, with the objective of determining the optimal mix of assets for your portfolio to properly withstand—and adjust to—changing market conditions. Usually, that means branching out among the three main asset classes—stocks, bonds, and cash. The difference between diversification and asset allocation is that the former is the "macro" big-picture theme and the latter is the "micro" nuts-and-bolts theme to building your mutual fund. Yes, you should diversify your portfolio. But how you do that is what's known as asset allocation.

That's just one facet of asset allocation you should know about. It's also important to draw a distinction between asset allocation and stock selection. The latter is choosing which asset to buy or sell, compared to others of the same type (or within the same asset class). For example, deciding whether to buy a corporate bond or a growth stock would be an asset allocation decision. Deciding whether to buy IBM or Caterpillar is a security selection decision because both stocks are in the same asset class: large-cap U.S. growth stocks.

Want to try another angle? Think of asset allocation as organizing your closet or your wardrobe. Unless you're a Minnesota Vikings fan you probably don't want all the shirts in your closet to be purple, right? No, you want to build a closet that reflects your eclectic clothing tastes in a vast rainbow of hues and colors. It's the same with your mutual fund. You want a personal portfolio that provides a diversified blend of asset classes that, ideally, produce higher potential returns while simultaneously doing a better job of managing risk.

Taking the analogy to another level, think of your investments as plants. Your growth stocks are roses; your value stocks are azaleas; your bonds are cabbage plants. Each "plant" is going to react differently to the investment "climate" depending on weather conditions. When the economy is sunny and warm, roses will fare better than cabbages. Conversely, when conditions are harsh and rain pelts the ground on a regular basis the hardy cabbage plant will do better than the rose.

The underlying principle behind asset allocation is no secret. History has demonstrated that asset classes don't move in lockstep. That means that, in any given period, large-cap stocks, small-cap stocks, international stocks, and U.S. Treasury bonds, to name a few, are moving up and down simultaneously. If you expect your portfolio to move in harmony like Fred Astaire and Ginger Rogers dancing on the silver screen you're going to be severely disappointed, not to mention on the road to financial ruin. Then there's the volatility angle. The fact is that stocks are much more volatile than bonds. Sure, they offer the prospects of larger returns, but, as recent history has shown us, stocks can plummet much lower and much longer than bonds over the long haul.

No, the idea is to build a mix of asset classes into your personal portfolio that takes your personal financial needs—your risk levels, your investment timeline, and your age, just to name three factors—and builds a proper (for you) asset allocation strategy around them.

The trick is to create the right balance of different stocks and different bonds to ensure that at least some of them are performing optimally at a given time.

The Importance of Asset Allocation

Having an asset allocation strategy isn't a luxury; it's a necessity. Studies show that over 90 percent of portfolio performance isn't attributable to one's legendary stock-picking skills or the addition of that high-flying financial advisor. Actually, the biggest factor in portfolio performance is asset allocation—how you set up your portfolio. Perhaps the best-known study on asset allocation and performance was done by Gary P. Brinson, Brian D. Singer, and Gilbert L. Beebower in 1991. Their conclusion was that considering commissions and other transaction costs, taxes, and mistakes, over 91 percent of long-term portfolio performance is derived from the decisions made regarding asset allocation. They broke down the factors that influence portfolio performance in this way:

Asset Allocation	91.5 percent
Security Selection	4.6 percent
Market Timing	2.6 percent
Other	1.8 percent

An Asset Allocation Backgrounder

Ever hear the name Harry Markowitz? Me neither, until I began my research for this book.

Back in the 1950s, Mr. Markowitz was a University of Chicago graduate student in economics who was wracking his brain over what to write his dissertation about. (I guess the mathematical chances of the Cubs winning the World Series were too depressing to contemplate.)

So, what does he do? After a chance encounter with a stockbroker, Markowitz began looking into what is now called Modern Portfolio Theory, which is just "egghead-esc" for asset allocation. Markowitz took the idea of building investment portfolios using different asset classes and ran with it. He, along with his friend William Sharp, honed the idea of asset allocation and how it could boost performance so well that, by 1990, the Nobel Prize people came calling. Today, asset allocation is as much a Wall Street staple as yellow power ties and hungover traders.

Your Asset Allocation Strategy

To build a personal portfolio using asset allocation, you need a well-crafted plan. Begin by taking a look at your investment goals, your tolerance for risk, and what kinds of investments you like to own.

Perhaps the best way to do that is by knowing what *not* to do. For instance:

Don't excessively duplicate—We discussed this in Chapter 4, but duplicating investments is just as important here. Don't fill your personal mutual fund with only energy stocks, or only small-company stocks. It's a recipe for disaster when, as always happens, energy and small-company stocks nosedive. Try to balance things out with some large-cap stocks, or some manufacturing company stocks, for example. That will ensure your portfolio still has some highs even if others are low.

Don't be "too" anything—As your mother said, "Everything in moderation." Don't be too aggressive or too passive. Try to build a blend of stocks and bonds that works for you. Experts call that an "all weather" portfolio. Sounds good to me.

Don't feel obligated to follow the herd—I know, everyone wants to be on the ground floor of the next Dell Computer or Raytheon. The trouble with that notion is 100 million Americans feel the same way you do. So if a hot tip comes out, chances are you're not the only one to know it (unless you know something the rest of us don't—in which case the SEC wants to talk to you). The problem with hot stocks is that you're usually buying them at the high and not the low. And buying high is not the strategy you're aiming for. Besides, a scattershot "hot stock" portfolio strategy is light-years away from a good asset allocation strategy: one that picks stocks for your portfolio based on your needs, risks, and goals, and the underlying company's ability to grow and make you more money over the long haul.

Don't forget to consider your own situation in life—nobody knows your personal financial situation as you do (another advantage, by the way, of building your own mutual fund). So build an asset allocation model that leans much more heavily toward stocks if you're ten years away from taking the gold watch and moving on into retirement. Keep it to 80 percent or more—you'll need to earn more money from your investments because, chances are, you'll be living a lot longer in retirement. Likewise if you're ten years away from a big life-time event, like a child going off to college, keep most of your money in stocks as well. Again, accumulating wealth—and not preserving it—is the goal when you have time on your hands. As you get within five years or fewer of your retirement or your child's college days, you can begin preserving the capital you've accumulated by investing in bonds. Remember, it's all about finding the right balance.

Don't limit yourself geographically—Your portfolio should act as a musical symphony with each stock (instruments) in beautiful accompaniment with the others. Take a world view, too, when choosing the "instruments" that will comprise your personal portfolio. Since the U.S. stock market comprises only about 50 percent of the world's financial markets, it only makes sense to add some international flavor to your fund. Consequently, deciding how much of your fund should be reserved for U.S. stocks and how much of it is reserved for foreign stocks is a good strategy to take. From 2000 to 2002, international markets, by and large, outperformed U.S. stocks. And it wasn't the first time, either. Some investors may feel comfortable with 10 percent of their portfolio earmarked for foreign stocks while others may say 20 percent or even 30 percent is a better bet. Either way, just make sure you include the rest of the world when building your fund.

Sample Asset Allocation Portfolios

Aggressive Portfolio
Stocks = 90 percent
Bonds = 10 percent
Cash = 0 percent

If you're young, you might just get away with being this aggressive. If you lose money when stocks go down, time is on your side. You have thirty years or more to make up your losses. But what happens if you have this type of asset allocation strategy at age fifty or fifty-five? Good luck trying to rebuild your portfolio in just five or ten years.

Moderately Aggressive Portfolio
Stocks = 75 percent
Bonds = 25 percent
Cash = 0 percent

A good mix of assets for those in their thirties or forties, or for those who started investing at a later age and need to catch up, though the latter group still faces too much risk for my blood.

Moderate Portfolio
Stocks = 60 percent
Bonds = 35 percent
Cash = 5 percent

If you're in your fifties and are near retirement, this could be a good blueprint to use. You're in your peak earning years, but you don't want to risk losing all the money you've invested by a sharply declining stock market. That explains the bond "padding."

Passive Portfolio
Stocks = 45 percent
Bonds = 45 percent
Cash = 10 percent

If you're already in retirement, this strategy could work. The fact is that most Americans who reach retirement age can expect to live another twenty or thirty years. So you can't get too conservative and load up on capital preservation investments like bonds. Even at sixty-five or so, you still need your portfolio to grow. That explains the stock "padding."

An Ongoing Process

When you begin picking the sectors that will comprise your personal portfolio, which is exactly what you're doing with an asset allocation program, think of it as a process rather than a singular event.

Why? Simply because the distribution of assets in your portfolio will probably ebb and flow along with the rest of the asset classes that comprise the stock market. An upward spike in the stock market could see your 80 percent stock and 20 percent bond allocation become 90 percent stocks and 10 percent bonds. To thwart having your portfolio go off-kilter, check in with your asset allocation level once or twice a year. ❖

Does Dollar Cost Averaging Work?

Ever hear of Dollar Cost Averaging (DCA)? It's a hot-button issue with Wall Street types who can't seem to decide whether DCA is a good idea or not.

In a nutshell, DCA is a systematic investment program where you put a set number of dollars into your portfolio on a regular schedule—usually every month.

The theory behind DCA is that if you put $100 into your portfolio every month, you're not only investing in the market on a regular basis (which is good), but you're also able to buy more stocks when the market is low and less when the market is high (which is better).

For example, let's say you set aside $100 every month to buy shares of Microsoft. If Microsoft stock is at $50, you can buy two shares of stock per month. But if Microsoft is trading at $25, then your $100 buys you four shares of stock per month. The point is that no matter what the market is doing, you always have your money working for you with DCA, and there's always something to be said for that.

But does DCA really work? I'm not so sure, especially if you already have a good asset allocation program in place. The problem is that DCA doesn't work very well when you're trying to diversify your portfolio. Yes, you can use DCA to buy one company's stock per month (probably even two) or invest in one mutual fund every month. But you're really not getting the full value of the entire stock market that way, are you?

The point isn't to take a small amount of money and invest it all in one place over a regularly scheduled timeline. The point should be to invest regularly, but along the parameters of a predetermined asset allocation program. So, if you have an asset allocation program that calls for 25 percent large-cap stocks, 25 percent small-cap stocks, 25 percent corporate bonds, and 25 percent cash, use the money you set aside for DCA every month to invest in stocks and bonds that meet your asset allocation needs.

The Relationship Between Asset Allocation and Risk

Building your own personal portfolio using asset allocation is a worthy goal, but it won't work out too well if you don't apply the lessons we've already learned about risk to the process.

That's because of the three primary asset classes—stocks, bonds, and money market securities—stocks historically provide the most risk, followed by bonds and money markets. But when you start talking about performance, you have to flip that order in reverse to find that stocks also offer the highest chance of investment returns, followed again by stocks, bonds, and money markets.

Average performance of stocks, bonds and cash investments—1926–2002 (annualized)
Stocks—10.6 percent
Bonds—5.2 percent
Money Markets—3.8 percent
Source: Ibbotson Associates.

That said, you rarely lose money—at least the kind of money you can lose on investing in stocks—when you invest in bonds or money market instruments. For example, stocks lost 43.3 percent in 1932, the largest decline in the equity markets ever recorded. Even recent history shows that stocks can be as volatile as the most temperamental diva at the Metropolitan Opera House. Over an eighteen-month period from 2000 to 2001, stocks lost 37 percent on average, as measured by the Standard & Poor's 500 Index. Compare that to five-year government bonds, which have never lost more than 5.1 percent in any calendar year.

The trouble is you don't make as much money investing in bonds as you do in stocks. Consider the following statistics from Ibbotson:

Between 1926 and 2002, stocks have outperformed both bonds and money market funds in:

- 79 percent of all five-year time frames.
- 85 percent of all ten-year time frames.
- 98 percent of all twenty-year time frames.

Finding the Right Balance

So what mix of stocks, bonds, and cash is right for you? Well, a blend of 40 percent stocks and 60 percent stocks would have earned, on average, 8.7 percent from 1926 through 2001, according to Vanguard, the mutual fund company. Not double-digit growth, but not bad, either.

Here's a look at how some sample allocations would have panned out over the same time frame, again from the Vanguard Group:

Portfolio #	Sample Allocations	Average Annual Returns	Worst 1-Year Loss 1926–2001
1.	Stocks—10%; Bonds—80%; Cash—10%	6.2%	-6.7%
2.	Stocks—20%; Bonds—80%	7.0%	-10.1%
3.	Stocks—40%; Bonds—60%	8.1%	-18.4%
4.	Stocks—50%; Bonds—50%	8.7%	-22.5%

PORTFOLIO # (CONTINUED)	SAMPLE ALLOCATIONS	AVERAGE ANNUAL RETURNS	WORST 1-YEAR LOSS 1926–2001
5.	Stocks—60%; Bonds—40%	9.1%	-26.6%
6.	Stocks—80%; Bonds—20%	10.0%	-34.9%
7.	Stocks—100%	10.7%	-43.1%

The meaning of these numbers harkens back, once again, to the earlier chapter on risk. Specifically, they ask the all-important question: How much money can you afford to potentially lose before you begin losing sleep at night?

In the Vanguard chart, if you build a personal portfolio that consists of 80 percent stocks or 100 percent stocks, can you accept the possibility of losing 34.9 percent or 43.1 percent of your portfolio in a given year?

True, we've all had experience losing vast sums of money in the financial markets. Three years of big losses in a row from 2000 through 2002 taught us that lesson. Oh, the pain!

But history shows us that, historically, stocks outperform bonds in the long run and that's a good starting point when deciding on an asset allocation strategy.

Take this scenario: If you had $1 invested in large-company stocks, it would have earned you $1,114 by the end of 1995, even though large-cap stocks lost money in twenty of those seventy years. Conversely, if you had invested $1 in Treasury bills over the same period (with only one down year for T-bills in that time frame), you only would have earned $12.87.

$1,114 to $12.87. That's the difference between capital accumulation (through stocks) and capital preservation (through bonds). But that's exactly why a good asset allocation program can help you when you're building your own mutual fund. Maybe the reason the calm investor can remain calm is that he's cushioned his personal portfolio with a smattering of stocks and money market investments to "protect" his exposure to risk he's undertaken with the stock section of his portfolio. That's the beauty of asset allocation—it levels the playing field over the long run without negatively impacting the portfolio's performance.

To sum up, let's pinpoint five specific steps you can take to create the best asset allocation strategy for you:

Investment goals—The first step in the asset allocation process is something you've already done by now—determined how much money you're going to need for retirement and for your other long-term financial goals. Then you estimate what kind of investment returns you're going to need to reach those goals.

Time horizon—Time horizon harkens back to the importance of starting early. If you start building your portfolio at age twenty-five, you're going to have a lot more time to weather those inevitable market declines. At age fifty, your shorter time horizon calls for more of a conservative asset allocation strategy. Let's face it, you likely don't have the time to compensate for a 30-percent loss in your portfolio in your fifties.

Risk—Can you live with periodic market losses that can deplete your personal portfolio by tens of thousands of dollars at a time? If so, congratulations, you've got a cast-iron stomach that a heavyweight boxer would envy. You can also afford to think more aggressively and that's really the best way to make more money in the investing game. But if the thought of losing $20,000 or $30,000 over the course of a year—as many Americans did in the early 2000s—gives you the vapors, then you have to decide if the 7- or 8-percent returns a year you'll get by weighting your portfolio down with some T-bills or Treasuries is worth it.

Financial situation—Have you created a budget? Do you have emergency cash reserves (experts recommend having six months of your annual income stashed away in cash for emergencies). Do you have big bills on the way, like college costs or a bigger mortgage? How close are you to retirement? Don't bother with an aggressive investment portfolio if you're going to need to get your hands on some cash in the near future. Your personal financial situation will dictate what your asset allocation program will look like.

Diversify—When I say "diversify," that doesn't mean you need one of everything. One useful rule of thumb is that the more money you have on hand to invest, the broader your investment choices must be. Typically, you can build a solid personal portfolio with as few as four or five asset classes. But feel free to go higher if you want to.

One more note: If you really can't bear the thought of investing in emerging market stocks or high-technology stocks, then don't. The absence of one or two asset classes from your portfolio really won't negate performance. On the contrary, the added comfort you'll gain by not investing in an asset class that only gives you the heebie-jeebies is worth any mediocre gains you might miss out on.

Folios and Asset Allocation

Most folio companies have designed their products with asset allocation in mind. Quick & Reilly, for example, allows its customers to set asset allocation goals for their own folios. Customers simply indicate how they want to be allocated within their folio and the company will automatically send their funds to the allocation they've designated. Changing and rebalancing the asset allocation levels within a folio is all up to the customer, though.

I've been saying all along that the best way to build your own mutual fund is by working with a folio company. Asset allocation is a good example of that. If, for example, you wanted to buy $2,500 worth of IBM to balance out the large-cap portion of your portfolio, it might take you a while to do so. After all, not everyone has $2,500 lying around these days. Even worse, by having a broker execute the order all at once you may be buying the entire lot at a time when the stock price is at a high.

With folios, you can ease gradually to such a position by buying bits of IBM along the way. Not only do you save yourself from a big cash hit, perhaps when you can't afford one, you're also investing more dollars when the share price has been trending lower, and fewer dollars when the share price is higher. Even better, you're not stuck with the fat brokerage fees you'd incur by accumulating shares of IBM gradually. Remember, most trades on folio accounts are free (up to a certain point).

Folios are also, by their inherent nature, particularly beneficial to an asset allocation program. Remember when I said that folios were "baskets" of stocks, each holding up to 50 or 100 individual stocks? That's important because it is much easier to build a diversified portfolio stock by stock than it is through an index fund or a mutual fund, where other factors besides your exposure to risk can hold sway.

Plus, with folios, you can more easily focus on one or more specific market segments and own stocks in those segments that have been researched and evaluated (by the folio company) using sound fundamental and technical analysis. Again, most asset allocation studies say that over 90 percent of a given portfolio's performance is due to asset allocation.

Case Study: *Spreading the Risk*

Carly Kane was brand-new to the folio world, but she was already loving every minute of it.

She loved the fact that she could pick her own stocks and make her own decisions, although she usually ran them by a financial planner first.

But when her planner told Carly that she was too heavily weighted in volatile technology and telecommunications stocks, she had to step back and take another look at her portfolio.

"My husband and my sister both work for tech firms and I did too before I settled down to have children," she says.

"So, yes, I lean toward technology stocks more than others because I know the industry and have full confidence in its ability to break new ground and make money for its investors."

Carly learned from her planner that while investing in an industry she knew so well was to her benefit, she was also placing her portfolio in a higher risk category by owning so many technology stocks. "Once he explained to me that I was too heavily weighted in technology stocks I knew what to do," she says. "I went right out and researched some good stable stocks in the utilities and consumer goods industries. I wound up selling my shares in Gateway and Nortel and replaced them with Pepsi-Cola and Boston Edison."

Carly says she felt better immediately. "I vowed never to keep so much of my money in one industry or one asset class. I'm glad I could figure asset allocation out before I got burnt."

Carly Kane Personal Portfolio
ALLOCATION PERCENTAGES
25% large-cap growth stocks
25% income stocks
25% small-cap growth stocks
25% high-grade corporate bonds
FOLIO FAVORITES
Home Depot, BellSouth, Cisco

Chapter Checklist

✓ Along with risk tolerance and diversification, asset allocation is a key issue in formulating your personal portfolio.

✓ Asset allocation means investing across a variety of asset classes, with the objective of determining the optimal mix of assets for your portfolio to properly withstand—and adjust to—changing market conditions.

✓ How important is asset allocation? So important that it accounts for over 90 percent of portfolio performance, experts say.

✓ When you begin developing an asset allocation strategy, keep in mind that, historically, stocks outperform all other investment classes.

✓ Most folio companies will help you develop an asset allocation strategy.

Chapter 7

Building the Perfect Portfolio

"Wealth is better than poverty—if only for financial reasons."
—WOODY ALLEN

In the late 1990s Americans turned Wall Street upside down. In the early 2000s Wall Street returned the favor.

Companies like WorldCom, Enron, Adelphia, and others that didn't make products that people actually use were the darlings of Wall Street. Companies like Procter & Gamble, General Foods, and IBM that *did* make products people actually use were relatively overlooked by investors, who only had eyes for stocks that possessed the one quality that investors value over all else—opportunity. Specifically, the opportunity for investors to get rich quick.

"Irrational exuberance," Federal Reserve Board Chairman Alan Greenspan called it. His words proved prescient as the dot-com industry and its wildly overinflated stock prices imploded, struck down by business plans that emphasized share prices over earnings.

Why this little trip down memory lane? Because when it comes to picking good solid stocks for your personal portfolio, it's strictly the basics that count. That means earnings, profits, steady growth, and good management. It doesn't mean which company has the most foosball tables or has the best Super Bowl commercials. Those were the "hot" companies that took their eyes off the ball, spending the bulk of their time not on creating and improving their products and services, but on finding new ways of keeping their stock price soaring. Investors in those companies paid a terrible price.

That leads us to the first rule of picking good stocks: Don't focus on the price of the stock; focus on the potential of the company. If a company can take care of its core business and build great products and services, the stock price will take care of itself. Back in the late 1990s, investors had it the other way around. They forgot about the basics and honed in on company stock prices. Recent history has shown us that they paid a severe price for doing so.

The second rule is to be as informed as possible before selecting the stocks you want for your portfolio. Digging up some good information on a company and knowing what to do with that information in the financial markets will give you a tremendous edge over the majority of investors who are content to get their market information from news headlines or from Sid down the hall in accounting.

Take your time when you set out to choose the stocks you want for your mutual fund. Believe me, there's no rush. You probably won't hear your stockbroker say this, but a good stock today is likely going to be a good stock tomorrow. So don't fling yourself willy-nilly into a stock pick you may regret after only a cursory review of its financial record. Take the time you need to get the story straight. Doing so can make all the difference in the world.

Can You Time the Market?

Financier Philip Fisher once said, "It's a good deal easier to know what's going to happen than when it's going to happen."

That train of thought should be the operating principle behind your stock research campaign. Sure, it's tempting to try to time the market and get in on a good stock that's just beginning to take off. But, as study after study has demonstrated, it's very difficult to time the markets. In fact, jumping in and out of the stock market may be the worst single thing you can do when building your own mutual fund. Why? Because if you're sitting on the sidelines waiting for the right time to get in again you could easily miss the moment when momentum swings upward again. Yes, you could get back in later but how much did you lose by being on the sidelines in the first place?

The answer is "plenty." In a study published in the *Financial Analyst Journal* that compared the results between market timing and buy-and-hold strategies from 1926 through 1999, researchers found that buy-and-hold outperforms market timing a whopping 98.8 percent of the time. Those are pretty good odds.

Yes, there is a time to sell your investments, but, by and large, history smiles on those savvy investors who pick a good stock or two and stay with it over the long haul. Your odds of making money are excellent and you'll probably sleep better at night knowing you've done your homework, found the stocks you like, and are content to let the stock do the rest of the work.

How good are your chances of making money in the stock market? The first few years of the twenty-first century notwithstanding, they're great. Take a look at the odds of making money in the stock market compared to the odds of some other life events to get a clear picture of why stocks are a good bet (the list of odds is from the Forum for Investor Advice):

- Odds that you'll win the lottery: 1 in 4,000,000.
- Odds that you'll be dealt a royal flush: 1 in 650,000.
- Odds that the earth will be struck by a meteor during your lifetime: 1 in 9,000.
- Odds that you'll be robbed this year: 1 in 500.
- Odds that the airlines will lose your luggage: 1 in 186.
- Odds that you'll be audited by the IRS: 1 in 100.
- Odds that you'll get snake eyes when rolling the dice: 1 in 36.
- Odds that you'll go to Disney World this year: 1 in 10.

- Odds that the next bottled water you buy is only tap water: 2 in 10.
- Odds that you'll eat out today: 5 in 10.
- Odds that an investment in stocks will make money in any given year: 7 in 10.

As the chart indicates, you have a 70 percent chance of making money in the stock market. Contrast that number to the odds of winning the lottery or being dealt a royal flush and you begin to understand why I keep harping about the importance of picking the right ones.

The Pitfalls of Market Timing

There's no shortage of studies comparing buy-and-hold investing with market timing. One of the best studies I've seen was commissioned by Towneley Capital Management and conducted by Professor H. Nejat Seyhun of the University of Michigan. This study calculated the effect of being invested in the stock market 100 percent of the time (as a buy-and-hold investor would) and being out of the market during days when the market rose. The findings are here:

PERIOD OF INVESTMENT	% OF TIME INVESTED	AVERAGE ANNUAL RETURN
Full 1,276 trading days	100%	26.3%
Minus the 10 best days	99%	18.3%
Minus the 20 best days	98%	13.1%
Minus the 30 best days	98%	8.5%
Minus the 40 best days	97%	4.3%

Source: Towneley Capital Management.

What You Should Know about Stocks

Investment guru Benjamin Graham's idea of investing was to buy $1 of value for 50 cents, over and over again.

Make no mistake, stocks give you the best chance to do just that. While bonds and money markets have their benefits, they can't compete with stocks performance-wise.

Let's take a brief look at stocks.

As mentioned earlier, stocks come in two varieties: common and preferred. In each case, when you buy a share of a given company, that means you own that company—even if it's only a single share.

Common stock may or may not pay dividends; preferred stock, because it gives investors first crack at a company's dividends, is generally bought for the income it produces, rather than the chance that the price will go up. Dividends are drawing more attention these days as Congress looks for ways to increase dividend payments to investors.

Stock Research Tips

Consider buying stock in companies that have had their earnings rise in each of the last three years by 25 percent or more.

Stay away from bargain basement stocks. Instead, focus on higher quality stocks selling at $15 a share and higher.❖

What Fuels a Stock's Growth?

Stocks are like newborn babies. With good nurturing, good parenting, and a good network of support, they'll grow and grow and grow. In the case of company stock, factors like good earnings, good sales growth, good management, and a good brand name make all the difference in the world.

But how do these factors translate into market growth? Let's have a look:

• **Earnings Growth**—Net earnings indicate whether a company has been successful in its mission to make money for its shareholders. The growth of those earnings often indicates whether the stock price will appreciate in the near future. A stock's earnings for the past three years, the present year, the last quarter, and an estimate of future earnings are all factors.

Questions to ask: Check a company's history. How has the company grown? What has the growth rate been? How fast are the competitors growing? What is a reasonable expectation for sales growth over the next five years?

• **Sales Growth**—You want to make a comparison between a stock's sales growth rate over the past year and its average growth rate for the previous three years. It's usually a positive sign if the sales growth rate for the past year is higher than the average of those for the past three years.

Questions to ask: Sales growth potential is a key determinant in stock forecasting. So ask whether company growth will come from new products, geographic expansion, or acquisition? What are the challenges to growth?

• **Price/Earnings Ratio (P/E) and Price/Earnings Growth Ratio (P/EG)**—The Price/Earnings ratio is the price of a stock divided by its earnings per share. It tells you how much investors are paying for a company's earning power. The P/EG is the P/E divided by the earnings growth rate. These two factors are important in helping you decide whether a stock is overpriced or underpriced. In general, the higher the P/E ratio, the more "expensive" the stock is (meaning overvalued in the market).

Questions to ask: Professional traders will tell you that P/E ratios are affected by growth expectations. Ask if it's common for an industry leader to have higher P/E ratios relative to its competitors? How have P/E ratios looked over the long haul? Are low P/E levels misleading? Sometimes a low P/E ratio may reflect a decline in stock price, but it's possible that new earnings reports will provide a different story.

• **Earnings Per Share (EPS)**—Earnings Per Share is the portion of a company's profit allocated to each outstanding share of common stock. That is to say, it's calculated by taking the earnings left over after all expenses and taxes are paid, and then dividing by the number of shares outstanding. This is a vital piece of information, as it can indicate how well the company is performing, and signals its return on investment.

Questions to ask: It's imperative that the company you invest in makes profits and will continue to do so. That was the downfall of the dot-com crowd as investors focused more on share price than on profits. Ask yourself, what is the likelihood that the company will make profits over the next few years? Compare the profitability of any company to its peers. Can you envision continued profitability with this firm? If not, you may want to take a pass.

- **Dividend Yield**—The annual cash return on a stock, called a dividend, is important to investors looking for income.

Questions to ask: Does the company pay a dividend? That's a good sign—it means the company generates a lot of cash and is less likely to pull an Enron or a WorldCom and build through our next factor, debt.

- **Debt**—A high level of debt may make it difficult for a company to withstand a period of financial or market difficulties. When you examine debt, zero in on the company's balance sheet. The stronger, the better. Long-term debt is bad. Short-term debt is worse. Low debt is best. Look for a company with no debt on the balance sheet. That means the company can take advantage of more vulnerable, debt-heavy competitors that share its marketplace.

Questions to ask: Stay away from companies with a lot of debt on their balance sheets. They're more trouble than they're worth. Ask how much debt has the company in question taken on? What's its plan for paying down that debt?

- **Capitalization**—Companies like Coca-Cola or Ford Motor Company with a large capital base usually have the resources to overcome periods of financial or market troubles. Consequently, they afford a certain level of safety to investors.

Questions to ask: What is the firm's market capitalization? Usually, large-cap companies have steadier, more predictable growth. Some say that small-cap companies are more nimble and adept at succeeding in today's global information economy. You wouldn't know it by the sector's track record in recent years.

- **Management**—Another key factor is strong management. Examine the histories of the company's top managers. Are they promoted from within or hired from outside the company? (Insiders are better—they know the picture inside and out.)

Questions to ask: How long has management been in place? Are they investors in the company? (They'd better be.) Is there a succession plan in place for the long term? Does management buy back company stock on a regular basis? (If they do, it usually means they believe in the company's growth prospects.)

Two more areas that I consider to be crucial barometers of a company's financial success are industry and geography. Specifically, what business is the company in? If it's in a prominent industry, like manufacturing or defense, those can be considered cyclical industries. By and large, if the industry isn't performing well, the companies that operate within the confines of that industry will struggle, too. Master of the obvious, right? But Wall Street is littered with the carcasses of investors who went against the grain and plowed money into a company in a sector that was gasping for air. Maybe it was a hot tip or maybe the investor liked the management team (which is another good area for determining the health of a company). But, more often than not, if a sector is a nonperformer, then the companies inside it are, too.

What's the old real estate mantra? That's right "Location, location, location." So companies that operate in countries with less onerous rules and regulations, especially in the areas of taxes and trade, may be better bets than similar companies in countries that may engage in over-regulation and potentially limit a company's growth. The same idea holds true for U.S. companies. State by state, company rules and regulations vary. Georgia, for example, will do all it can to keep Coca-Cola happy. But does Massachusetts feel the same way about Raytheon or Bose? It's an issue well worth looking into.

The Value of Stock Ownership

Simply stated, stocks grow much higher than other investments. Take a look:

If you invested $1 in the following asset categories in 1926, it would have been worth this much by 2000:

- Small-company stocks—$5,520
- Large-company stocks—$1,828
- Long-term government bonds—$39
- Treasury bills—$14

Stock-Picking Advice

Some additional ways of picking the right stocks for your personal mutual fund:

- Go with the best. Buy the top-selling company in an industry in earnings and sales growth, profit margins, and product quality.
- Hone in on companies that emphasize management ownership of stock.
- Always look for stocks that consistently meet and beat market expectations.
- Fluctuate cash reserves. Take profits when stocks are at a premium, to take advantage of market corrections.
- If a stock moves significantly lower after you make a purchase, don't worry. In fact, add to your position as long as the fundamentals of the stock remain positive.
- To reduce market risk, keep a diversified portfolio of eight to twelve stocks from various industries. Increase your position in growth stocks that perform well over time and meet or beat market expectations.

- Use market volatility and dips as buying opportunities.
- Adopt a strategy that considers stock valuation to be important but understands that historical multiples do not apply to many new economy stocks. In other words, Wall Street really hasn't figured out how to valuate new economy (i.e., dot-com, biotech, telecom) stocks.
- Always keep a level head and watch market conditions. Don't be overpositioned in any given sector when the market signals otherwise.

Mistakes to Avoid

It was Homer the Poet who said that true reward was in the trying and not the succeeding. But it was Homer the Simpson who said trying was the first step to failure.

While we strive to emulate the former more than the latter, sometimes stuff happens in our efforts to select the best stocks for our personal portfolios. That's okay. Stock-picking, like most endeavors, is a learning process. And we all learn from our mistakes. But wouldn't it help to know in advance the mistakes *others* have made so you don't have to make them yourself?

That's the idea behind this section—an overview of some of the more common—and painful—stock research mistakes Americans make. Learn them, live them, love them. Just don't make them:

1. **Overconfidence**—Some may even call it arrogance. (Hey, I just did!) It's human nature to think we know more than the next guy, unless the next guy has a stock tip you hadn't heard about. Put it this way. You could take every guy who had a hot stock tip that didn't pan out and fill every football stadium in America—and probably Europe, too.

2. **Thinking short term**—You're watching a football game. Your team's quarterback fumbles. *Arrgh!* Short term, you're not feeling so confident. But as the game develops, your team's

quarterback makes a few key passes and leads his team to victory. That's a long-term gain, so to speak. Investing is the same way. Too often we're focused on the short term at the expense of the long term. But focusing on the short term can lead to ill-advised panicky moves. It can also increase your trading costs, since you're trading so much to improve your portfolio position. And trading too often is not what you want to be doing with your own mutual fund. Remember, it's all about picking the right investments in the first place and having the security and confidence to let them do their job over the long term.

3. **Selling the wrong stocks**—The stock market is a volatile environment. One moment you're up and the next you're down. And people—being flesh-and-blood human beings—just can't stand seeing their stocks go down. So they sell them. The lesson here is that volatility happens and you're not going to be able to escape it. So again, pick the stocks that are right for you and hang in there if there is some short-term volatility that decreases the value of your stock for a while. That said, if there's a long stretch where your stock is in decline, by all means sell it. (See Chapter 8 for more on when to sell.)

4. **Being stubborn**—Okay, I know. This sounds contradictory after what I just finished telling you about selling winners. But even after our best efforts, some of the stocks we pick for our personal portfolios may, for one reason or another, not pan out. Don't be afraid to swallow your pride and jettison a loser if it becomes painfully evident that the stock is—and will likely remain—a loser.

5. **Not doing your homework**—This mistake harkens back to Mistake #1, in that it's always easier to act on someone else's information rather than on your own. But think about that. Would you buy a car from someone who picked it out for you? I wouldn't. That ugly tie or awful sweater you got from your well-intentioned mother-in-law for Christmas last year? Wouldn't you have preferred to have some input? That's the key here. Going out and doing as much research on your own as you can and then making a suitable investment decision is

infinitely wiser and has a bigger payoff than listening to the idea of the guy down the block of what makes a good stock for you.

6. **Not having a plan**—You'd be amazed but studies show that about half of all Americans don't have an investing plan. That's why the first chapters of this book spent so much time on budgeting, goal setting, and knowing your financial needs. After all, you plan for your vacation, you plan for your career, and you plan for your diet and health. Why should your finances be any different?

7. **Buying on the cheap**—Too often we can't resist a bargain. That habit may not translate into too much trouble at garage sales and flea markets, but it can really decimate your investment portfolio. Why? Because if you scour the countryside for cheap stocks on the premise that they have the most opportunity for growth, you're forgetting one of the most important investment rules out there—buying quality. Remember, you want companies that lead their industry, that make money year after year, that have great management. Unfortunately, those stocks usually don't come cheap.

Look for Diversity and Stability

Look around with an eye for diversity. Your mutual fund should represent six to eight different industries or asset classes. And try not to put more than 20 percent in one stock. Conversely, don't have more than one or two stock positions at less than 5 percent. At that level, the stock's performance won't have much impact on your performance. Of course, feel free to "test drive" one or two stocks with small positions to see if you want to expand them in your portfolio.

Another tip: Look for companies that show promise for the long haul. I know, that's not easy to do.

But if you apply the factors that we've been discussing in this chapter—earnings, management, industry ranking, profits, and stability—you have a good chance of finding the next

General Electric. When you do, think about this fact: One share of GE purchased in 1928 grew to $65,000 in value by 2000.

Becoming an Intuitive Stock Picker

I hail from Boston, Massachusetts: home of beans, cod, the Red Sox, and Adams Media, the publisher of this book. Also calling Boston home is investment industry legend Peter Lynch, former manager of Fidelity Investments' high-flying Magellan Fund.

Lynch really has a way of communicating with investors that most Wall Street gurus don't have. He's a true people guy. For instance, his advice on choosing stocks is short on mathematical models and analysis spreadsheets that are so favored by many in the investment industry. Instead, he advises going down to the local shopping mall or grocery store and watching what people are buying. Or watching what stores have the most foot traffic.

For a mutual fund guru, Lynch is a big fan of having YOU make the ultimate investment decisions. You decide what your investment time frame is. You decide the risk you're going to take with your portfolio. You choose the stocks that work for you and not necessarily the other guy whose goals and needs probably don't match your own.

He's also a big advocate of another investment strategy I like—portfolio testing. What this means is you go ahead and plunk down an imaginary $5,000 or $10,000 in a "test" portfolio to see how it does for a while. Most folio companies have such testing capabilities and they've proven very popular with investors who want to take their new folios out for a drive without the commitment of buying them.

Here are some more pearls of wisdom on stock selection from the great Peter Lynch, as he provided in his book *Beating the Street*, written with John Rothchild (Simon & Schuster, 1993). All are well worth knowing:

- Firms in slow-growth sectors like utilities or waste management are often written off by investors as unglamorous investments in mundane industries. But think about it. Lynch says that "mundaneness" can limit the competition and increase chances for growth. He cites Superior Industries, which makes wheels for the automobile industry, as a good example, rising 719 percent from 1985 to 1992.

- Firms that create products people have to keep buying like soft drinks and toothpaste will always have a market. Lynch cites Coca-Cola and Gillette as solid, long-term performers, since folks still have a soft drink or need to shave during a recession.

- Firms with sales growth but lousy earnings. Lynch advises not confusing the two. It's possible for a company to do well in sales and growth of sales revenue, but still not make money. Sales growth doesn't drive a company's value; earnings drive long-term growth.

- Firms with a niche in their market or industry may do well in the long term if their fundamentals are strong. Lynch cites Southwest Airlines, a stock that rose 701 percent between 1990 and 1998.

- Firms with strong balance sheets—if ten stocks are in an industry that is losing money, the two with good balance sheets should outlast the eight in heavy debt. To locate such companies, Lynch advises finding their annual reports either directly from companies or on the Web.

A Word on Investment Psychology and "Bubbles"

The reason that Peter Lynch proved to be such an excellent stock picker is that he understood people—specifically how they view money and their chances of making it in the stock market.

For a stock picker, there's no greater characteristic to have. Let's face it, as much as we'd like to make our investment decisions with the cold calculation of a computer chip, our emotions and our behaviors often won't let us. As the technology bubble of the late 1990s demonstrated, it's easier and less complicated to follow the herd than to do our homework and get a reliable barometer on a stock's potential direction. But when the bubble burst, investors learned a lesson in financial behavior they'll never forget.

In the prehistoric days of the 1990s, when dot-com millionaires walked the earth and a single share of some Internet stocks sold for about the same price as a new microwave oven or a round of golf at Pebble Beach, few investors wanted to hear about bubbles. Perhaps that's why when the technology bubble finally burst in 2000, so many investors were carried away by the herd, unable to sell their dot-com stocks and technology funds before it was too late.

Why the trouble with bubbles and what does financial behavior have to do with it?

First, a short lesson on bubbles: Financial market bubbles happen when stocks rise in price, regardless of fundamental factors such as earnings or revenues. As a result, valuations of companies ballooned to vastly overinflated levels. That's exactly what we saw in the dot-com gold rush of the late 1990s, when many highly regarded Wall Street analysts were hard-pressed to properly valuate technology companies but still proceeded to predict they would rise to $200, $300, and even $400 per share. Chasing the dream and ignoring the bubble, investors stampeded toward technology stocks with a vengeance, pushing stock prices up to historic levels and setting the stage for the technology bubble burst of 2000 in the process.

The technology bubble of the late 1990s—like most market bubbles—had three stages. First, there was a shift in market psychology, driven by the Internet craze. Next, the share prices of technology companies rose until their valuations reached speculative heights. Then IPOs (initial public offerings, remember?) were floated to soak up capital. Before long, we saw IPOs that represented little more than a set of ideas and people in a prospectus. The notion of making products that people actually use, à la Procter & Gamble or Ford Motor Company, was viewed as quaint by many investors. Once that rationale set in, the bubble burst.

Such a return to more realistic stock prices is not unusual. Here's a chart on occasions in recent history when the market fell back to Earth.

Average Length of Market Corrections over the Last 35 Years

START OF CORRECTION	LENGTH OF CORRECTION	+1 MONTH	+3 MONTHS	+12 MONTHS	% OF RETURN AFTER END OF CORRECTION
Nov. 1968	14 months	-22.0%	5.0%	-4.1%	12.8%
Jan. 1973	21 months	-48.0%	119.0%	113.0%	38.0%
Oct. 1987	2 weeks	-31.4%	6.7%	10.8%	23.1%
Jul. 1990	3 months	-19.9%	6.2%	6.7%	29.1%
Feb. 1994	2 months	-8.9%	2.9%	1.7%	15.1%
Jul. 1998	3 months	-19.2%	18.9%	32.9%	39.3%
Apr. 2000	21 months	+3.4%	+5.8%	N/A	N/A

Behavioral Finance

We've all heard of the herd mentality, right? The most recent market bubble in 2000 was a classic case of everyone following the herd—right off a cliff. There, the enthusiasm for technology stocks and the sustained bull market was based on the shaky premise that everyone was buying, so everyone bought.

The herd mentality is just one unfortunate byproduct of what many investment strategists are now referring to as "behavioral finance."

Behavioral finance studies the intersection of psychology and finance, concentrating on behaviors that may affect investment decisions and security market prices in ways that few can predict. These behaviors are, strictly speaking, not rational, in the sense that they will probably lead to losses rather than gains. Behavioral finance deals with mistakes. And not just the random kind of mistakes that are inevitable from time to time, but systematic mistakes that investors tend to make again and again. The reason for these mistakes, it is proposed, is the nature of the human mind.

That's the theoretical model. In practice, behavioral finance works like this. If enough irrational people are willing to pay ridiculously high prices for stocks, then the prices of such stocks, as we saw in 1998 and 1999, will go up. Seeing these prices go up and wanting in, more irrational investors will follow the trail and buy as well. In such a sequence, stock patterns emerge from common human behavior.

The problem with investors who practice "behavioral" tendencies is that, by and large, they disregard dreary performance indicators like earnings estimates, price-earnings ratios, and revenue growth, in favor of emotional motivators. What cool new e-commerce company did the guy in the next cubicle just buy? What hot dot-com stock is your butcher touting?

Investors who suspect they invest emotionally should ask themselves if they really want to get their market advice from their butcher. Rib roast, yes. Growth companies, no.

Identifying the Stages of Behavioral Finance

Are you prone to behavioral investment tendencies?

It's not difficult to find out. As behavioral finance has become a more prominent issue on Wall Street (and on Main Street, too), human behavioral experts are beginning to crack the code and figure out what exactly happens to investors who succumb to the herd mentality and replace logic with emotion when making investment decisions.

One of the better efforts originates from Woody Dorsey, a behavioral market expert and president of the research firm Market Semiotics. A forecaster and publisher of research for institutional investors based on behavioral methodologies, Dorsey used the technology bubble of the late 1990s to identify the stages of investor psychology (as follows):

- **Mania:** Investors displayed absolute optimism during the dot-com bubble, reaching a peak in the first quarter of 2000. Dorsey coined the mania as "E*Greed" in December 1999.
- **Denial:** Investors ignored reality, convinced there was a problem just with tech stocks and not with the broad market. They were in denial of the bear market.
- **Hope:** Investor expectation that recovery was a "sure thing" due to the "EZ-Street" concept of Federal Reserve easing. That hope peaked in May 2001.
- **Recognition:** Investors finally face the reality of a declining economy and dropping stock prices. This recognition was accelerated by the events of September 11.
- **Reprieve:** Stocks "bounce" as investors assume the worst is over and believe the market "must" recover because it is "oversold." Dorsey says we are nearing reprieve now.
- **Liquidation:** Massive selling as investors finally "get out" of equities. The final stage of liquidation is panic selling or capitulation, which allows the market to enter a new bull cycle.

Source: "The Semiotic Stages of Bear Market Behavior," copyright 2001 by Woody Dorsey of Market Semiotics (www.marketsemiotics.com).

Other behavioral experts are quick to point out tendencies that investors make under the guise of behavioral finance. If you are more confident than you should be in your forecasting ability, do not process information efficiently, experience the illusion of control, give undo credence to management and research gurus, and hang on and even add to losing positions, you might just be a "behavioral" investor.

The Blueprint for Success?

What to do about it? Several useful suggestions have been advanced to help investors deal with behavioral impediments to investment success. Here's a list of habits to learn that can separate you from the herd:

1. Accept that investing is the art of probabilities, not certainties.
2. Recognize and avoid the circumstances leading to undue confidence.
3. Deliberately seek out the contrary view.
4. Have a written plan for each position, especially the "exit strategies."
5. Create feedback loops with your financial advisor that allow for process analysis and improvement.

Also, try not to give too much weight to recent experience. Try some self-examination, too. People often see other people's decisions as the result of disposition but they see their own choices as rational. And remember that the stock market is a leading indicator. Thus, much of what you read in the print and online media has already been discounted in stock prices.

Overall, try to be critical when times are good, opportunistic when times are bad, and aware enough to leave emotion, passion, infatuation, or antipathy out of the investment process.

Adopting a long-term, diversified investment plan may be your best defense against many of the behavioral tendencies discussed here. A properly constructed portfolio will contain a number of different investments, each fulfilling a particular role or niche contained in the plan. Although each piece may be more or less risky than the others, your primary consideration should be on the much larger and more important long-term objectives of your overall portfolio.

That kind of behavior bypasses bubbles and creates wealth.

Web Heaven: Places to Go on the Internet to Research Stocks

I love the Web, and in this I'm no different from most other Americans. The World Wide Web is the single biggest reason that self-empowerment books like this can even be written. The great equalizer, the Internet, offers investment research that ten years ago was the sole domain of the big brokerage firms and mutual fund houses. Now it's all yours. Try these investment research sites out and you'll see what I'm talking about:

• *www.cnbc.com*—Offers real-time investment news for serious investors.

• *www.aaii.com*—Has bulletins from the *Journal of the American Association of Individual Investors* on issues like building logical stock screens, devising a contrarian strategy, and learning how tax-law changes affect IRA options.

• *www.bloomberg.com*—Has a wealth of online news and market updates as well as features from *Bloomberg Personal* magazine.

• *www.msn.com*—A great site from Microsoft that features one of my favorite financial writers, Mary Rowland. It also gives you advice from traders and money managers, provides updates on stocks in the news, and guides you to related financial subjects such as online banking.

- *www.edgar-online.com*—Source of SEC filings and related business intelligence.
- *www.hoovers.com*—Source of company information and late-breaking news.
- *www.motleyfool.com*—Featuring the Fool's yuk-a-minute market commentary, the site is a solid investment site for beginners as well as savvy market pros. It has company message boards, updates on Dow theories, and features such as the Daily Double and Daily Trouble, which single out stocks that have recently doubled or been halved in price.
- *www.thestreet.com*—Includes Jim Cramer's brash commentary, value plays on low-priced stocks, and information on what mutual fund managers are buying and selling.
- *www.vanguard.com*—Offers the Investor Education University, a huge collection of educational resources focused on mutual fund investors.
- *http://CBSMarketwatch.com*—A disclaimer. I've written for this site. That said, it's still one of the most useful places on the Web for straight, no-nonsense investment advice.

Case Study: *Doing the Homework*

Bob Keane—known affectionately by his customers at the pub he owns near Wilmington, North Carolina, as "Buffalo Bob"—just came into a pile of money from an inheritance.

Wanting to put the money right to work, Bob plowed about $15,000 into his personal portfolio, primarily to beef up some positions he was starting to feel were underweighted.

"I began doing some homework and checking up on some companies I thought had a good chance for growth," he says. "I'd been loading up on *Fortune* 500 stocks and felt I was beginning to miss out on some growth opportunities."

Keane started by looking into one of his favorite sectors, biotech, to see if there wasn't a good fit for him there. "I found a company that had already received a patent for a new diabetes drug and which had received $500,000 in new financing," he says. "It was trading at $8 when I found it and had already gone up to $9.50 in the three days it took me to get all the information I needed to buy it."

Focusing on the company's financial history, including its earnings and sales figures over the five years it had been in existence, Keane decided to go ahead and buy the stock. "What really convinced me was the fact that the stock had outperformed analyst expectations every year. That sold me right there."

By doing his homework, Buffalo Bob had significantly increased his chances of finding a winner.

Bob Keane Personal Portfolio
ALLOCATION PERCENTAGES
10% growth and income stocks
20% aggressive growth stocks
20% mid-cap stocks
30% equity income stocks
20% life insurance variable annuity
FOLIO FAVORITES
Coca-Cola, Eli Lilly,
Federal Home Loan Mortgage Corporation

Chapter Checklist

✓ When it comes to picking good solid stocks for your personal portfolio, it's strictly the basics that count. That means earnings, profits, steady growth, and good management.
✓ Studies show that timing the markets—getting in when it's low and out when it's high—is nearly impossible. A buy-and-hold strategy beats market timing nearly every time.
✓ Get to know your stocks by doing solid research. Focus on earnings, profits, management, and industry rank, for starters.
✓ Overconfidence and thinking short term are sure ways to lose money in your personal portfolio.

## Chapter 8

How to Trade in Stocks

"Be not afraid of going slowly; be only afraid of standing still."
—CHINESE PROVERB

N ow it's time to put your plan into action. Or, as my father used to say when he'd spend all day out in the cold stringing up Christmas lights, "It's time to flip the switch."

If you've made it this far, you're as prepared as you're ever going to be. You've set your goals, evaluated your risk, studied your asset allocation angles, and researched the stocks and bonds you want to include in your personal portfolio. Now it's time to go out and build that portfolio and start managing it. That's what this chapter is about.

First things first. If you build your own mutual fund through a folio company, they'll walk you through the process of executing a trade. Even so, it's a good idea to know how to buy and sell stocks, what kinds of trades and orders you can place, and how to do it all from your own personal computer.

Trading Online

That last part is important. Wall Street has come a long way from the days when eighteenth-century merchant bankers would send stock tips to customers via carrier pigeons.

Thanks to the World Wide Web, vastly superior stock market trading executions are now available to a broader base of customers—not just the $1 million and up crowd. But you have to have a PC with a fast connection to the Internet to take advantage of trading online.

In most cases getting online is easier than ever. Prices for personal computers have sunk so low that computer makers are practically giving them away. For about $600 you can get a fully loaded personal computer that can easily handle your portfolio trading needs. To hedge against rapid obsolescence, spend a little bit more to get a PC with at least 32 megabytes of RAM (Random Access Memory), although 64 MB would be even better. Also make sure you're running a computer that has a fast and reliable processor (the computer "chip" is the brains of your PC). Machines running Intel's Pentium chip should suffice.

Your connection to the Internet should be fast and reliable. The best options are broadband cable modems or Digital Subscriber Lines (DSL). Most Internet users use the traditional dial-up lines that companies like AOL offer subscribers. Dial-up may be fine if you're only going online to swap recipes with Aunt Melba, but it's not the way to go if you're going to be trading stocks. Dial-up lines are slow and unreliable. You don't want your Internet connection to go dead when you're trying to dump 1,000 shares of that telecom company whose CEO was just seen on CNBC being led away in handcuffs.

Be Careful Out There

Care to go trolling on the Internet for some great stock tips? Fine by me. Just beware that the online "analyst" who says he's found the next eBay may be a paid tout for the very same stock he's promoting. Paid touts thrive in the murky underworld of stock-tip Web sites, where you don't have the opportunity to make eye contact and take the measure of a person. It's tempting—seemingly objective analysis from a reputable source who asks nothing in return for the great tip he's providing you. All you have to do is plunk down some money for the stock he's pumping and sit back and wait for the big payoff. By the time you've figured out that you've been duped, and that you need a microscope to locate what's left of your investment, the "analyst" is long gone, paid off handsomely by the same company executives who took your money and got out early.

Placing Your Order

In most cases, you'll be executing your trades online on a folio company's Web site. Remember, they're your best bet for handling your personal portfolio account. If you elect to build your own mutual fund via a discount broker, the story is pretty much the same (only more expensive). Both folio companies and discount brokers have the resources to provide you with real-time trading quotes and fast executions. After you've opened an account with them, you'll be provided with a user identification number and password that will allow you to access your account. When you buy or sell a stock through these sites, the company will immediately send you a confirmation notice either via e-mail or directly to your account letting you know that it received the order. Your account order screen will consist of a form that includes small "checklist" boxes, such as "buy" or "sell," the number of shares involved, stock symbol (more on that later), type of market order (ditto), and length of time for the order to be open. After you submit your order, you'll receive a message asking you to check your order over and make sure all the information is accurate. If not, the screen should have a "cancel" option allowing you to back out and start all over again. Or change your mind and walk away from the trade entirely if that's your wish. You'll need the "cancel" option, for example, if you enter a buy order for 1,000 shares of Disney when you only wanted to buy 100. Or if you *wanted* to buy 1,000 shares of Disney but changed your mind at the last minute.

Where Your Order Goes

After you place your order, it will be sent to a trading exchange for execution. Primarily, it goes to either the New

York Stock Exchange or to NASDAQ, the all-automated dealer exchange. In general, your order will be paired with a contrary order, meaning if you want to buy you'll be matched up with someone who wants to sell. If there's no counterpart, a market maker down on the trading floor will buy or sell your stock if nobody else will.

After Your Order Is Executed

After the transaction is completed, you'll receive another notice telling you the price you bought/sold at and the number of shares. Make sure these confirmation notices are also time stamped—you'll need that information if a discrepancy arises over the order and you start wrangling with the folks who placed your order.

More Than Just Trading

Most folio companies and discount brokers' Web sites also include charts and graphs and asset allocation models for you to play around with while you build your portfolio. ❖

Types of Orders

Depending on what kind of trade you want to place, you'll have to specify the type of order you want to accommodate your particular trading needs. Here are the most common types of stock market orders:

• **Day order**: A buy or sell order that expires at the end of the business day if it has not been executed. Say you wanted to buy Microsoft at $55 per share. But during the course of the day the stock price never sank that low. A day order lets you try again tomorrow.

GTC (Good 'Til Canceled): An order either to buy or to sell a stock that remains in effect until the customer cancels it or until it is executed. Some folio companies and/or discount brokers will cancel these orders after ninety days.

• **Limit order**: An order to buy or sell at a specified price or better. Limit orders enable you to set the price you will buy or sell a stock at. For example, you own Dell at $75—but you think the stock is going to $80. So you place a limit order to sell when Dell gets to $80. There is no guarantee that your limit order will ever be executed.

• **Market order**: An order that is to be executed immediately (or "on the hop" as they say on the trading floor). Market orders are executed at whatever price the stock is listed at the time your order reaches the trading floor. For example, say Nike is trading at $50 when you place your market order. Your purchase or sale of Nike will be very close or right at the $50 price level. Here is where real-time stock market quotes come in handy. Real-time quotes will give you a good idea of the price your order will be executed at. Working without real-time quotes is a bit like those dreams you have where you're standing naked in a crowd. In other words, it's a frightening experience.

• **Stop loss order**: An order that stands unexecuted until the stock trades at a specified price. Once the stock trades at the specified price, the order is executed and becomes an active market order. It's only to sell a stock at a rock-bottom price.

• **All or None (AON)**: A stipulation on a limit order either to buy or sell a stock only if the broker can fill the entire order and not part of it. If the order is not completely filled by the end of the business day, it is canceled. That means if you want 1,000 shares of AOL Time Warner Inc. but only 500 are available at your price level the trade—at your "All or None" request—will not be executed.

• **Fill-or-Kill**: A stipulation on a limit order either to buy or to sell a stock only if the broker can get an immediate execution. If it cannot be filled immediately, the order is automatically canceled. "Fill-or-Kills" are a good idea if you think you can get a stock at a good price. If the stock never hits your price, the order won't be filled.

How Stocks Are Priced

When you begin trading for your personal portfolio, you're going to hear the terms "bid" and "ask" a lot. You'll hear some other strange terms, too.

Not to worry. They're simply terms professional traders use to buy and sell stocks. They're easy to learn, too. Here's a description of the terms you'll need to know:

- **Bid**—When you're looking to sell stock, the bid is the highest price someone will pay (often a market maker down on one of the trading exchanges) to buy the stock from you.
- **Ask**—When you're buying stock, the ask is the lowest price someone will sell you the stock for.
- **Volume**—The number of shares traded in a certain stock.
- **Open**—The price at which a stock is trading at the start of the trading day.
- **Close**—The price at which a stock is trading at the end of a trading day.

A Sample Stock Quote
STOCK: AMERICAN BROOM COMPANY (ABC)

Price: 45.8125	Bid Size: 20	Open: 43.00
Change: +2.8125	Bid: 45.75	High: 46.00
Volume: 1,440,750	Ask: 45.8125	Low: 42.8125
Exchange: New York	Ask Size: 26	PE Ratio: 86.5
Year High: 48.250	Year Low: 35.8125	

Understanding Stock Symbols

Before you place your orders, make sure you understand stock symbols. Millions of dollars have been lost because lackadaisical investors wrote the wrong stock symbol on their trade order. It's a careless but common mistake, one I saw made many times during my years on Wall Street. Fortunately, it's easily avoided if you know your symbols.

Stock ticker symbols have a pedigree that any Vanderbilt would be proud of. Ticker symbols appeared in 1844, shortly after the introduction of the telegraph machine. Wall Street fell in love with the symbols immediately, as stock prices could be transmitted by brokers in seconds instead of days. Full names of companies were used at first, but that proved unwieldy. Frustrated wire operators began transmitting stock prices with the company name in shorthand, and a revolution was born.

About twenty-five years later, just after the Civil War ended, the first stock ticker machine began clacking away in New York City. At the turn of the century, newspapers began tracking stock prices via ticker symbols on their business pages. A millennium later, you can still find stock tickers in newspapers. But it's also generated electronically online on business Web sites like The Motley Fool, CBSMarketwatch, and a host of others.

Here's how stock symbols work. Each stock traded on global exchanges is identified by a short symbol. For example, the symbol for Citigroup is "C." Similar abbreviations are used for stock options, mutual funds, and many other securities.

Stock symbols are designated by one, two, three, or more letters for a reason. A ticker with three letters or fewer indicates the company trades on the New York or American exchanges. Tickers with four or five letters trade on the NASDAQ, NASDAQ Small Cap, or OTC Bulletin Board markets.

When you run into a stock ticker symbol with five letters, there's usually a story behind the company. If, for example, a stock ticker symbol has an "E" at the end of its name, it's considered by the Securities and Exchange Commission to be delinquent in filing key regulatory documents. A "Q" tells a more troubling story—it's the scarlet letter that tells investors a company is in bankruptcy proceedings.

Understanding Stock Tables

Once you know what stock symbol to look for, the next step is to go onto the World Wide Web or open your daily newspaper's business section and find your stock table. It will look something like this:

A Typical Stock Table, Explained
THURSDAY, MARCH 10, 2003
XYZ Corporation

52 Weeks/ Hi-Lo	Sym	Div	Vol	Yld	P/E	Close	Change
$47–$37	ABC	230	335	5	10	$39.50	+$1

- **(52 Weeks/Hi-Lo) 52-Week Hi and Low:** The highest and lowest prices that a stock has traded at over the last year.
- **(Sym) Ticker Symbol:** The alphabet-soup name that identifies the stock on the exchange that the stock is traded on. Most tickers on World Wide Web investment Web sites will give you the option of locating a stock by company name or by sticker symbol.
- **(Div) Dividend Per Share:** This means the annual dividend payment per share.
- **(Vol) Trading Volume:** The total amount of shares traded for the day, listed in hundreds.
- **(Yld) Dividend Yield:** The percentage return for the dividend. The dividend yield is listed as annual dividends per share divided by price per share.
- **(P/E) Price/Earnings Ratio:** P/E is calculated by dividing the current stock price by earnings per share from the last four quarters.
- **(Close) Daily Close:** The close is the last trading price recorded when the market closed on the day.
- **(Change) Net Change:** The dollar-value change in the stock price from the previous day's closing price.

Get Your Quotes on the Web

Nowadays, it's far more convenient for most people to get stock quotes off the Internet. This method is superior because most sites update throughout the day and give you more information, news, charting, research, and so forth.

To get quotes, simply enter the ticker symbol into the quote box of any major financial site like CNBC.com, Yahoo Finance, CBS Marketwatch, or MSN Moneycentral.

Benchmark It

When you buy a stock, you're more than likely buying a stock that's included in one of the main market indexes. These indexes are important for a variety of reasons—they make it easy to categorize types of stocks and also make them easy to follow—but the best reason is that they offer a benchmark against which to match the performance of your stock. Here are the most prominent indexes:

- **The Dow Jones Industrial Average**—The granddaddy of stock market indexes and the one that's followed by most investors. This index tracks thirty large-cap stocks, including heavy hitters like General Electric, Ford Motor, Home Depot, and Wal-Mart.
- **Standard & Poor's 500**—The index the pros use. The S&P 500 is widely used by trading firms because it follows a much larger number of stocks. This index tracks 500 of the roughly 7,000 publicly traded stocks in the United States.
- **NASDAQ Composite**—A value-weighted listing of the nearly 5,000 stocks listed on the NASDAQ. The NASDAQ Composite mostly tracks technology stocks. The NASDAQ was riding high during the glory days of 1998 but fell on hard times as tech stocks dove off a cliff in the early 2000s.
- **Russell 2000**—The Russell 2000 follows 2,000 small company stocks. If you're into small-cap growth companies, this is the index to compare your portfolio against.

- **Wilshire 5000**—The Wilshire 5000 monitors all 7,000 publicly traded stocks in the United States. A broad index, true, but a good indicator of how the market views stocks at any given time.

- **Lehman Government/Corporate Bond Index**—The LGCBI is composed of government and investment-grade corporate bonds with maturities of one to ten years.

- **MSCI-EAFE**—The Morgan Stanley Capital International–Europe, Australia Far East Index follows about 1,000 of the largest stocks in Europe and Pacific Basin markets. A great index if your portfolio has an overseas component.

- **Solomon Brothers World Bond Index**—The SBWBI follows bond investments, primarily in Europe.

What's a Good Stock Portfolio?

A good stock portfolio is any portfolio that is built with your best financial interests in mind. It should include stable, well-managed companies and include a growth component to take advantage of market upswings. A portfolio should also have some capital preservation element, like Treasury or corporate bonds, to safeguard your wealth in the event of a market decline. The most important element is that the portfolio is customized with you in mind, taking into account your goals, your needs, and your risk comfort levels.

Sample Stock Portfolios

Here are a few sample stock portfolios from the folks at FOLIO*fn*. Notice how some are indexed to certain categories (like large-cap or small-cap stocks and some are mixed):

FOLIOfn's Dow Jones 30 Portfolio

#	Symbol	Company	Weight (% of Folio)
1.	AA	ALCOA INC	1.78%
2.	AXP	AMERICAN EXPRESS CO	2.89%
3.	BA	BOEING CO	2.61%
4.	C	CITIGROUP INC	3.04%
5.	CAT	CATERPILLAR INC DEL	3.73%
6.	DD	DU PONT E I DE NEMOURS & CO	3.36%
7.	DIS	DISNEY WALT CO DISNEY	2.45%
8.	EK	EASTMAN KODAK CO	2.70%
9.	GE	GENERAL ELEC CO	1.96%
10.	GM	GENERAL MTRS CORP	3.18%
11.	HD	HOME DEPOT INC	1.80%
12.	HON	HONEYWELL INTL INC	1.02%
13.	HPQ	HEWLETT PACKARD CO	1.61%
14.	IBM	INTERNATIONAL BUSINESS MACHS	6.64%
15.	INTC	INTEL CORP	1.37%
16.	IP	INTL PAPER CO	3.04%
17.	JNJ	JOHNSON & JOHNSON	4.49%
18.	JPM	J P MORGAN CHASE & CO	2.06%
19.	KO	COCA COLA CO	3.60%
20.	MCD	MCDONALDS CORP	1.23%
21.	MMM	3M COMPANY	10.57%
22.	MO	PHILIP MORRIS COS INC	3.24%
23.	MRK	MERCK & CO INC	4.53%
24.	MSFT	MICROSOFT CORP	4.28%
25.	PG	PROCTER & GAMBLE CO	7.00%
26.	SBC	SBC COMMUNICATIONS INC	2.09%
27.	T	AT&T CORP	1.68%
28.	UTX	UNITED TECHNOLOGIES CORP	5.36%
29.	WMT	WAL-MART STORES INC	3.98%
30.	XOM	EXXON MOBIL CORP	2.74%

FOLIOfn Global Portfolio

#	Symbol	Company	Weight (% of Folio)
1.	AIG	AMERICAN INTL GROUP INC	2.00%
2.	AVE	AVENTIS ADR	2.00%
3.	AZN	ASTRAZENECA PLC ADR	2.00%
4.	BAC	BANK OF AMERICA CORPORATION	2.00%
5.	BCS	BARCLAYS PLC ADR	2.00%
6.	BP	BP AMOCO P L C ADR	2.00%
7.	BRK.A	BERKSHIRE HATHAWAY INC DEL CL A	2.00%
8.	C	CITIGROUP INC	2.00%
9.	CHL	CHINA MOBILE HONG KONG LTD ADR	2.00%
10.	CSCO	CISCO SYS INC	2.00%
11.	CVX	CHEVRONTEXACO CORP	2.00%
12.	DELL	DELL COMPUTER CORP	2.00%
13.	DT	DEUTSCHE TELEKOM AG ADR	2.00%
14.	E	ENI S P A ADR	2.00%
15.	FMX	FOMENTO ECONOMICO MEXICANO SA ADR UNITS	2.00%
16.	FNM	FEDERAL NATL MTG ASSN	2.00%
17.	GE	GENERAL ELEC CO	2.00%
18.	GSK	GLAXOSMITHKLINE PLC SPONSORED ADR	2.00%
19.	HBC	HSBC HLDGS PLC ADR NEW	2.00%
20.	HD	HOME DEPOT INC	2.00%
21.	HMC	HONDA MOTOR LTD AMERN SHS	2.00%
22.	IBM	INTERNATIONAL BUSINESS MACHS	2.00%
23.	INTC	INTEL CORP	2.00%
24.	JNJ	JOHNSON & JOHNSON	2.00%
25.	KO	COCA COLA CO	2.00%
26.	LYG	LLOYDS TSB GROUP PLC ADR	2.00%

FOLIOfn Global Portfolio (continued)

#	Symbol	Company	Weight (% of Folio)
27.	MO	PHILIP MORRIS COS INC	2.00%
28.	MRK	MERCK & CO INC	2.00%
29.	MSFT	MICROSOFT CORP	2.00%
30.	MTF	MITSUBISHI TOKYO FINL GROUP ADR	2.00%
31.	NOK	NOKIA CORP ADR	2.00%
32.	NTT	NIPPON TELEG & TEL CORP ADR	2.00%
33.	NVS	NOVARTIS A G ADR	2.00%
34.	PEP	PEPSICO INC	2.00%
35.	PFE	PFIZER INC	2.00%
36.	PG	PROCTER & GAMBLE CO	2.00%
37.	PTR	PETROCHINA CO LTD ADR	2.00%
38.	RD	ROYAL DUTCH PETE CO NY REG GLD1.25	2.00%
39.	SBC	SBC COMMUNICATIONS INC	2.00%
40.	SI	SIEMENS A G	2.00%
41.	SNE	SONY CORP ADR NEW	2.00%
42.	TLS	TELSTRA CORP LTD ADR FINAL	2.00%
43.	TM	TOYOTA MOTOR CORP SP ADR REP2COM	2.00%
44.	TSM	TAIWAN SEMICONDUCTOR MFG LTD ADR	2.00%
45.	UPS	UNITED PARCEL SERVICE INC CL B	2.00%
46.	VOD	VODAFONE GROUP PLC ADR	2.00%
47.	VZ	VERIZON COMMUNICATIONS INC.	2.00%
48.	WFC	WELLS FARGO & CO NEW	2.00%
49.	WMT	WAL-MART STORES INC	2.00%
50.	XOM	EXXON MOBIL CORP	2.00%

Folio FN Analysts Choice Folio

#	Symbol	Company	Weight (% of Folio)
1.	ABC	AMERISOURCEBERGEN CORP COM CL A	3.33%
2.	ABT	ABBOTT LABS	3.33%
3.	AIG	AMERICAN INTL GROUP INC	3.34%
4.	AMGN	AMGEN INC	3.33%
5.	APA	APACHE CORP	3.33%
6.	ATH	ANTHEM INC	3.33%
7.	C	CITIGROUP INC	3.33%
8.	CAH	CARDINAL HEALTH INC	3.33%
9.	CCU	CLEAR CHANNEL COMMUNICATIONS	3.33%
10.	CD	CENDANT CORP	3.33%
11.	CTX	CENTEX CORP	3.33%
12.	DHR	DANAHER CORP DEL	3.33%
13.	ERTS	ELECTRONIC ARTS INC	3.33%
14.	FNM	FEDERAL NATL MTG ASSN	3.33%
15.	FRE	FEDERAL HOME LN MTG CORP	3.33%
16.	HCA	HCA-HEALTHCARE COMPANY	3.33%
17.	HCR	MANOR CARE INC NEW	3.33%
18.	HIG	HARTFORD FINL SVCS GROUP INC	3.33%
19.	INTU	INTUIT	3.33%
20.	LOW	LOWES COS INC	3.33%
21.	MDT	MEDTRONIC INC	3.33%
22.	MSFT	MICROSOFT CORP	3.33%
23.	NKE	NIKE INC CL B	3.33%
24.	PFE	PFIZER INC	3.33%
25.	PG	PROCTER & GAMBLE CO	3.33%
26.	PX	PRAXAIR INC	3.33%
27.	THC	TENET HEALTHCARE CORP	3.33%
28.	UNH	UNITEDHEALTH GROUP	3.33%
29.	WFC	WELLS FARGO & CO NEW	3.33%
30.	WLP	WELLPOINT HEALTH NETWORK NEW	3.33%

These, of course, are folios that were selected by FOLIO*fn* as "Ready to Go" folios, and were not selected for a particular individual investor like you. But they should give you a good idea of how folios are constructed.

When Should You Sell?

So you've accumulated an all-star lineup of stocks for your personal portfolio. Unfortunately, a clunker or two found its way into your portfolio, too. You know you want to sell them—but when?

On the high seas, fishermen call it "cutting bait." In Las Vegas gaming palaces, gamblers call it "quitting while you're behind."

On Wall Street, traders call it "taking a loss—so you can gain profits."

Cutting your losses in any activity isn't easy. It's tough for fishermen to haul anchor after a day of empty nets. It's difficult to walk way from a poker table down $300. And it's particularly gut-wrenching to sell a favorite stock that, despite thorough research and the best intentions, is never going to earn a return on your investment. It's so difficult, in fact, that a recent study by finance expert Terrence Odeon, called "Are Investors Reluctant to Realize Their Losses?" shows that investors are twice as likely to sell their winners as their losers.

That said, on Wall Street, walking away from a poor investment could very well be the difference between a solid investment portfolio and a mediocre one. In fact, accepting the fact that you've latched on to a losing stock and selling it may be one of the keys to investment success.

Why Sell the Losers (When You Think They're Winners)?

Sure, selling a favorite stock is no picnic. It's an admission that your stock-picking skills aren't as formidable as you thought they were. But the price of not doing so is significant. As legendary investor Bernard Baruch once said, "Even being right three or four times out of ten should yield a person a fortune if they have the sense to cut losses quickly."

Letting go of your portfolio laggards is a fact of life. In the stock market, downturns happen so you have to protect your investments accordingly. The key is to make rational decisions—not rationalize ways of clinging to a portfolio-draining stock or mutual fund. Even if you bought the stock based on a well-respected Wall Street analyst's decision, don't hang on to it if it sinks like a stone in the briny deep. After all, nobody is immune to a bad investment.

Even if you believe in a stock so strongly that it breaks your heart to let it go, keeping a lid on what you lose is a good idea. Let's face it, there's no room for sentiment when it comes to your financial future. Dumping a loser requires you to look at the stock more objectively, without the emotional strings attached that led you to buy it in the first place. If you can't let go of the stock, consider this: Would you buy the security today at its current price? Are better investment options not available? Probably not.

For further proof let's look at the numbers. If you purchased a stock at $100 a share and it falls to $80, you've got problems. To get back to $100, the stock has to make a 25 percent gain. Or, if the stock drops 50 percent, to $50 a share, it would take a 100 percent bounce for the stock to reach $100 again. And who knows how long that will take—in the unlikely event it happens at all?

Why Cutting Losses Is a Good Idea

Here's a set of hypothetical trades to illustrate how cutting losses can boost your portfolio:

STOCK	SHARES	COST/ SHARE	SELL PRICE	PROFIT/ LOSS	% PROFIT/ LOSS
A	100	$50	$46	-$400	-8%
B	100	$43	$40	-$300	-7%
C	100	$57	$98	$4,100	+72%
D	50	$24	$22	-$100	-8%
E	30	$110	$101	-$279	-8%
F	70	$85	$78	-$490	-8%
G	100	$65	$79	$1,400	+22%
Total Profits and Losses			+$3,731		

As the numbers indicate, even if you had made these seven trades over a period of time—and taken losses on five of them—you would still finish up by more than $3,700. That's because the two stocks that worked out resulted in a combined profit of $5,500. And the five losses—all capped at 8 percent, except for one that was cut early at 7 percent— added up to $1,569.

Consequently, it would take several 8 percent losses to wipe out the profit from just one or two good stocks.

Tax Advantages of Taking an Investment Loss

While taxes aren't the only reason for selling a poor performing stock, they're a good one. That's because Uncle Sam has thrown investors a bone in the form of a tax code provision that allows you to use realized capital losses to offset any capital gains, or up to $3,000 in ordinary income. In simpler terms, you can take the losses today, still remain in the market, and use those losses to offset current capital gains—and future capital gains, if the loss is greater than 3,000, due to carryover rules.

As a result, you can sell an underperforming stock today and gain the tax benefit of the reduction in price in next year's tax bill. If you insist the shares have strong potential future appreciation, you can simply put the stock back after locking in the loss deduction.

If you do repurchase the stock, make sure you know the Internal Revenue Service "wash sale" rules. The IRS disallows any current deduction if you buy the stock either thirty days before or thirty days after the loss sale. So wait thirty-one days after your loss sale to escape this tax trap.

Free Up Your Portfolio for Better Things

Nine times out of ten, it's better to deep-six a stock that's underperforming. A quick look at the math confirms that sentiment: Given the fact that a stock that declines 50 percent means you will need to double your money to get back to even, keeping your losses in your portfolio is an uphill climb. Consequently, unburdening your portfolio of such laggards will allow it to grow in value more quickly and painlessly.

How to Act in a Declining Market

Selling an individual stock or two that are underperforming is one thing. But what happens when the entire market is tanking and threatening to take your portfolio down with it?

If that happens you have to ask yourself some questions. Does watching your portfolio go south cause your blood pressure to go north? Are you wallpapering the basement with worthless stock options? Does a bear market turn you into a grizzly, growling menace at home and at work?

Relax—you're in good company. Some 50 million investors feel the same pain you do. And remember, bear markets go into hibernation a lot sooner than you might think. The classic definition of a bear market—a 20-percent decline in average stock prices over a two-month period.

In the meantime, consider the following courses of action for investing your money in declining financial markets.

Do Nothing: That's right—nothing. Take a nap. Watch *The Sopranos*. Have a margarita. If you have a financial plan in place, perhaps the smartest thing to do in a tough market environment is to stay the course. The worse thing you can do is to jump out of the stock market because chances are you'll still be on the sidelines when the market picks up again. That's called "market timing" and, as we've already mentioned, even professional traders usually can't figure out when stocks will rise again. By remaining in the market, you'll be assured of being there when the market rebounds. You should sell if a stock falls 2 percent over two years (one, if you're antsy).

Go Sector Shopping—If you feel you must take some course of action, consider changing the stocks you're buying. Historically, some stock sectors do better than others in declining markets. For example, high-dividend stocks tend to be less volatile than other stocks. They are usually insulated from big bear-market drops due to the dividend alone. Sector-wise, utility stocks, consumer cyclicals, service-oriented companies, food stocks, and pharmaceutical stocks tend to do better during an economic downturn than other companies. Some stock sectors just tend to outperform others during a bear market. The bad news is that when the market does turn bearish again these stocks won't rise as fast and as high as, say, technology or emerging market stocks.

Diversify—Having a well-designed mix of investments is a great idea anytime, but especially so in a down market. That's because you don't take a pounding by having all your eggs in one potentially leaky basket. Studies show that holding a judicious mix of growth and value stocks, possibly in international as well as U.S. companies, and some bonds and cash investments too, is a great way to minimize investment loss.

Think Incrementally—and Keep Buying: Historically, stocks rebound much higher than their price levels just before a bear market. This was the case in both 1987 and 1990 during the last two bear markets. So by contributing regularly to your personal portfolio, you're "buying at the dip" as Wall Street traders like to say. That means you're buying when prices are low, thus giving you significantly more bang for your investment buck. Remember, stocks become overpriced as bull markets mature. They become cheap in bear markets.

Another potential move to make in a bear market is to place more money into fixed-income products like U.S. Treasury bonds and money market bonds. Just remember that by doing so you risk being on the sidelines when the stock market rebounds. And, if you don't already have one, consider consulting a financial advisor for tips on surviving a bear market. Usually, the first consultation is free.

Above all, stay calm. Bear markets tend to dissipate fairly quickly and bull markets last a lot longer. Think about that before you do anything rash with your (until recently) high-flying investment portfolio.

Tracking the Performance of Your Portfolio

Not to get too metaphysical but think of your personal portfolio as a journey rather than a destination. Take the trip, enjoy the scenery, and stop along the way once in a while to see what kind of progress you're making.

What does tracking your portfolio mean? More of what we talked about in Chapter 7. You know, the homework thing. Once you buy a stock, it's a bit like getting married. The more you know about your partner, the fewer surprises there are.

To keep things flowing smoothly, start tracking the stocks you purchased for your personal portfolio by keeping tabs on company news, earnings reports, and industry conditions. Pay special attention to things like changes in management, dividend announcements, stock buyback programs—in short anything that can impact the price of your stock. To make things easier, turn to the Internet again. There's no shortage of Web sites that will automatically notify you of developments at companies that you've included in your portfolio. Sites like PR Newswire *(www.prnewswrire.com)* or Hoover's *(www.hoovers. com)* will automatically keep you notified of such events.

From time to time, you'll need to rebalance your portfolio to keep your investment plan on track and keep your asset allocation framework in place.

Here are some other tips on keeping track of your personal portfolio:

- Review all documents that you receive from the firm that's handling your personal portfolio. Check to make sure your confirmations and account statements are accurate.
- Make sure you have all your trade confirmations and account activity sent to you and not to a financial advisor (if you have one). It's okay to share paperwork with a professional planner but make sure he or she gets the copies and you get the originals.
- Don't be shy. If you're unsure of anything related to the administration and maintenance of your portfolio, ask questions.
- Periodically, keep up-to-date on independent research on your investments. That means reading prospectuses, research reports, offering materials, annual reports (Form 10-K), quarterly reports (Form 10-Q), and other filings that a company makes with the SEC. SEC filings, such as Forms 10-K and 10-Q, can be accessed on the SEC Web site.
- Rebalance your personal portfolio as your financial circumstances change. As things change—your daughter gets married, you buy a second home, you retire early—you may have to change your portfolio's asset allocation.

The Tax Picture: How to Keep More of Your Own Money

The relationship between Wall Street and Congress has always been a tug of war over the amount of money made by investors on Wall Street and the amount of that sum that Uncle Sam deserves in taxes.

Wall Street would prefer that as little as possible of its investors' earnings be taxed. Congress doesn't see it that way, asking investors to dig into their pocketbooks and ante up some of the proceeds from their portfolio gains.

Just a case of some high-level give-and-take? Perhaps—but that's the way it's been for decades. While those two entities agree to disagree, what can you, the do-it-yourself investor do to hang on to your personal portfolio earnings?

The answer is that you can do plenty. First, you should know the lay of the land—namely, the types of investment taxes, such as capital gains or retirement plan taxes, and how they work. Then, once you know what the stakes are, it's up to you—and your tax preparer, if you have one—to craft a tax strategy that keeps more of your money in your pocket.

The Basics of Taxation

Taxes can be owed on a wide variety of investments, from Portuguese debentures to South African gold futures. Primarily, though, tax-related events occur on the purchase and sale of U.S. stocks, bonds, mutual funds, and other investments. They also happen when you invest in tax-deferred retirement vehicles such as IRAs and 401(k) plans. In addition, your house—which may be your biggest investment—is also affected by the tax code.

By and large, investment income is taxable in three areas: dividends, capital gains, and (investment) interest.

• **Dividends**—These are income distributions from a company's profits to its shareholders. Investors have the option of receiving the dividend in the form of a check or they can have the proceeds automatically reinvested in a dividend reinvestment plan (DRIP).

• **Capital gains and losses**—Each time you sell an investment security such as a stock or bond—or a piece of real estate—at a profit you generate a capital gain. When you sell at a loss, a capital loss is generated.

With a capital gain, the tax rate is determined by the holding period of the asset. A holding period is the length of time you own an asset—for instance, a stock, bond, or a money market investment. For holding periods of more than twelve months, the rate is now 10 percent for those in the 15 percent bracket and 20 percent for those in the other brackets. For an asset held less than twelve months, the capital gain is the same as ordinary income.

With a capital loss, long-term and short-term losses can be written off dollar for dollar against any capital gain.

• **Interest**—Interest earned from your investments, mostly fixed-income investments, is considered taxable at your marginal tax rate.

Despite a widespread belief that only mortgage interest is deductible, the law still allows investors to deduct interest on loans used to make investments. Such interest is deductible to the extent of your investment income. When totaling up your investment income for purposes of this limit, you generally can't count capital gains that get special treatment under the law. Congress doesn't want to let you deduct investment interest in a higher bracket if your gains are being taxed at only 10 or 20 percent. You have the option of including your capital gains in investment income but then cannot take advantage of the lower capital gains rates. Contact your tax professional for help in determining which option is best for you.

A Folio Tax Planning Strategy

The goal of any investment tax plan is to minimize your tax liability and maximize your gain. In other words, take all the investment trades you've made from January 1 to December 31, add their values as of year end, and you'll have your net gain or loss. For example, count up all your gains and losses for the year and write off the losses. If your losses totaled $11,000 for the year in the stock market and your gains totaled $10,000, you can write off $1,000 in losses.

In tax planning, just as in investing, timing is everything. So the idea is to separate your investment losses and stick Uncle Sam with a piece of the bill. If, for example, you have capital gains on investments where you've earned a profit, those gains may be offset by selling another security you own for a loss. You can do so by selling your investments at a loss before the end of the tax year (December 31) to give your trade a chance to settle before the year runs out, thus "timing" your sale to fully maximize your tax advantage. The idea is to deep-six your losers by December 31, particularly when your gains are higher. That move nets you a tidy deduction for your investment loss, plus you pay any taxes owed at a much lower rate.

The Importance of Holding Periods

As we mentioned earlier, the amount of tax you owe on a given investment is based on the length of time you owned it. In tax lingo, that's called a "holding period." The actual gain or loss is determined by comparing the asset's basis with its selling price, and the holding period helps determine the rate at which the gain is taxed—not the actual gain or loss itself. The IRS doesn't calculate holding periods starting January 1 of a given year. Instead, it starts the clock when you buy an investment. For instance, if you purchased 100 shares of General Electric on May 1 and sold it all the following April 30, that's a short-term taxable event. If you sell the stock on May 2 of the following year, the IRS considers that as a long-term gain or loss and will tax the sale at a lower tax rate.

Taxes and Your Folio Stocks

Good stock tax management depends on your ability to keep track of all your trades, particularly when you buy the stock of the same company at different times and at different prices. When you decide to sell some of the stock, being able to identify which shares to part with will permit you to control the tax consequences of the deal.

That's why it's important to know your basis for all of your stock transactions. The cost basis, in brief, is your investment in the property, the amount you will compare to the sales proceeds to determine the size of your gain or loss. The higher you can prove your basis to be, the less gain there is to be taxed . . . and therefore the lower your tax bill.

Consider this example. You bought 100 shares of ABC stock in January 2002 for $2,400 (including commission), giving you a basis of $24 per share. In January 2003, you purchased 100 more shares, this time for $2,800. Your basis in each share is $28. In January 2004, you purchased another 100 shares for $3,000, giving each share a basis of $30.

When the stock hits $40 a share in April 2004, you decide to sell 100 shares. If you simply tell your broker to sell 100 shares, the IRS FIFO rule (first in, first out) comes into play. It is assumed that the first shares you purchased—the 2002 group with the $24 basis—are the first ones sold. That would create a taxable gain of $16 a share or $1,600. But if you directed your broker to sell the shares purchased in 2004, with a $30 basis, the taxable gain will be $10 a share, or just $1,000 (assuming it's taxed at the 20 percent rate). The rate could be different based on your income, but the effect on your tax bill will still be positive.

In either case, you'll get $4,000 from the sale of the stock and because you've owned all the shares more than twelve months, your profit will get long-term gain treatment. But, your tax bill would be significantly different: $320 versus $200.

Folio Deductions to Take

As you create and manage your personal portfolio, are the investment-related expenses you incur along the way tax deductible? You bet.

Everything from the cost of calling your folio firm to the service charges you pay for your dividend redistribution plan are tax deductible.

Here's a short list of what you can deduct:

- The cost of investment magazines, newsletters, and books.

- The cost of trips to your financial advisor or stock-broker's office (if you have one).
- Investment fees, custodial fees, trust administration fees, and other expenses you paid to maintain your taxable investments.
- Fees for online trading (restricted to account maintenance-related fees).

Don't break out the champagne yet. All trading fees and commission still are not tax deductible, although they do reduce the tax basis of the security sold.

Case Study: *Cutting the Tax Bill*

Anne Ferguson couldn't figure out why she was spending so much on taxes for her mutual funds—especially when she was losing money every year.

"I just didn't understand why I had to pay taxes on my funds in years when performance was off."

As a marketing executive at a large biotech firm, Anne had access to some of the best accounting minds in the area. She buttonholed one tax expert at her firm and asked her to explain how she could get a better deal with folios over funds when it came to taxes.

"I didn't want to pull all my money out of my funds," she explained. "But I did want to conduct a bit of a laboratory experiment to see if I could do better in folios than I was doing in funds.

"I did not want to give up part of my investment returns to taxes on year-end capital gains distributions," she continued. "I figured that index mutual funds and folios were my best bets, but I soon found that only folios could do the trick."

Ferguson also wanted more than just tax efficiency. She also wanted to harvest her losses to offset other gains or income. "I found that outside of individual stocks, only folios allow selective tax-loss harvesting," she says. "Folio firms not only allow it, but they also make it very easy to do by including tax calculators in their programs."

Now Ferguson is happy to check in with her folio firm and find out whether she should make a move in her portfolio for tax reasons. "I have much more control over the tax portion of my investments with folios. It's enough to make me move all my money over into personal portfolios."

Anne Ferguson Personal Portfolio
ALLOCATION PERCENTAGES
20% aggressive growth stocks
20% equity income stocks
10% small-cap growth stocks
10% large-cap growth stocks
40% Treasury bonds
FOLIO FAVORITES
Bank One, Viacom, Pfizer

Chapter Checklist

✓ Make sure you have a fast, reliable computer.
✓ Get to know stock symbols and stock tables.
✓ Make sure you know the major stock indexes. They'll give you a reliable benchmark to compare your portfolio against.
✓ Know when to sell an underperforming stock.
✓ Rebalance as your financial situation changes.
✓ Get a grip on taxes and how they impact your folio.

Chapter 9

When You Need a Little Help

"Ask people's advice, but decide for yourself."
—Old Ukrainian proverb

P roffering advice to people who consider themselves "do-it-yourselfers" isn't easy. After all, Socrates spent his life traveling Ancient Greece advising the populace. And they poisoned him.

But, if you need a shoulder to lean (but hopefully not to cry) on as you manage your own mutual fund, help is available in the form of a financial advisor.

Most personal portfolio companies and discount brokers will make some form of professional financial advice available to their customers, if they want it. It's understandable why they may not. Individuals who build their own mutual funds want to be in the pilot's seat and want to be the one pulling the proverbial trigger and making the big decisions.

But like the president of the United States or the chief executive officer at IBM, making decisions with a knowledgeable expert or two on your team who has an "I got your back" mentality can be a big advantage. That's especially true in the investment game, where so many decisions are emotional and an objective analysis of your portfolio-picking strategy can really come in handy.

I know what you are thinking. "I thought that the whole idea was to build my own fund and not pay someone else to do it?" That's true. But try to remember that the real issue is control. With mutual funds you cede control over your financial decisions and don't make any yourself, apart from choosing to invest in the fund in the first place. That's just not so with personal portfolios. You make all the investment decisions. You pick the stocks that comprise your fund. You decide what types of asset allocation models you'll use. And you decide when to rebalance and when to buy or sell the stocks that make up your portfolio.

Still, there's something to be said for an experienced hand in your corner when the going gets tough. Think Burgess Meredith in *Rocky*. Or think Robert Duvall's *consigliore* character in *The Godfather*. These are the types of veteran observers who can provide wise counsel when you really need it. But in the end, you're the Sly Stallone or Marlon Brando character making the final call.

As it should be.

Folios and Financial Advice—A Rising Tide?

As more banks, brokerages, and yes, even mutual fund companies begin to develop personal portfolio programs of their own, we'll begin to see more folio programs that include some level of financial advice. Financial service firms like the idea of a new and exciting product that complements their existing product offerings. And they've also noticed how investors have grown just as excited about buying and trading personalized portfolios of stocks. They know what I've been telling you for the last eight chapters—that personal portfolios combine the simplicity and diversification of mutual funds with the control and tax savings of direct stock ownership.

With companies like E*Trade, Fidelity Investments, and Merrill Lynch all now offering some kind of personal portfolio program that comes with a financial advisory option, investors have more choices than ever about the level of financial assistance they may require. This may entail going it alone and building your own personal portfolio without the help of an advisor, or it may mean having an advisor choose the stocks that will comprise your folio for you (and just sitting back and reaping the fee and tax advantages of a personal portfolio over a mutual fund). Somewhere in the middle is perhaps the future of personal portfolios—a level of financial advisory services where a financial services professional will review your individual portfolio on a regular basis, but not with the same level of attention and service that Bill Gates or Donald Trump gets.

Why a Financial Advisor?

Why not?

A good financial advisor is worth it, unless you are so sure of what you're doing that you don't want anybody butting in with annoying advice about avoiding penny stocks or knowing what a company actually does before investing in it.

Cynical, am I? Maybe so. But let's at least look at some of the benefits you can derive from seeking a financial advisor's counsel.

They'll make it their business to know your financial goals—One of the first things you'll do when you hook up with a financial planner is fill out a questionnaire detailing your financial situation and what your investment objectives are. Then, if the advisor is any good, he or she (or they— sometimes financial advisors work in pairs or teams) will meet you face-to-face and draw enough of your financial personality out as they can. You want them to do this. That way, if retirement planning is your chief concern—they know it. If tax management is your priority—they know it. If it's making up for lost time because you didn't start investing until your forties—they know it. Then they can help you plan accordingly.

They'll help you create a plan to reach your financial goals–Once financial advisors get over the shock of you wanting to make all the final investment decisions, they may spend some time talking you out of it. You'll stand your ground and remind them that you want the control. They'll then sit down with you and develop a blueprint for contributing to your personal portfolio on a regular (say, monthly) basis. They'll help you develop an asset allocation program that is so well put together that you'll be able to work off it for the rest of your life. They'll even tell you how much money—to the dollar—that you should have invested in your folio at a given time. A good financial advisor wants you to do well because it means they're doing well on your behalf. That's why they take the time to learn your objectives, time horizon, and risk tolerances; offer asset allocation recommendations tailored to your individual needs; and help you reallocate your portfolio to meet changing needs; see the Zen happening here? Robinson Crusoe had his Friday and you have your financial advisor.

They understand the financial markets—Well, better than most folks, anyway. What I like about the financial advisors I know from my years trading and then covering Wall Street is that good financial planners understand the emotional side of investing. And that's important. Your worst enemy in building your own mutual fund is emotion—specifically, your emotions. A savvy financial advisor will help you stuff your emotional genie back into the bottle. Those 500 shares of that telecom stock your brother-in-law virtually guaranteed would double in price by June? Your financial advisor will talk you out of it by March. That move into auto stocks when consumer demand is way down? An advisor will ask you to think again. In short, a good financial advisor can save you from yourself.

They can help you build a portfolio that works for you— Few people understand how volatile the financial markets are more than a good financial advisor. Trust me, they've seen people make millions and lose millions in the markets and could tell you tales that would make your hair curl. That's okay. A financial advisor who's prone to war stories isn't such a bad thing. It's good to hear what volatility has done to other unfortunate souls, if it means you won't emulate their mistakes. Here, an advisor plays a mentorship, Yoda-like role that you can really use when you're managing your personal portfolio. In the words of Yoda, "Do not try. Do. Or do not."

They are a fountain of specific information—You may not know how that telecom industry stock has fared over the past five years, how much volatility it's undergone, how it has compared to other stocks in its category, how the stock has done in and up down markets, and what its price potential might be. But your financial advisor does. Financial advisors are good at debunking analyst reports and market rumors, too. That's the emotional issue again. They'll make sure that when you do make a big portfolio decision it will be made only after careful consideration and with solid judgment behind it.

They'll help you get information—Let's face it. You're busy with your career, your family, your life. You can't devote 24/7 to your investments. Who can? So when a particularly good opportunity arises—say a stock that fits your investment profile to a "tee"—you'll have a devoted ally looking out for your best interests who is plugged into the markets working on your behalf.

Do You Need a Financial Advisor?

Would you be better off with a financial advisor? Consider these factors:

- The amount of money you have.
- The complexity of your finances.
- How much of the investment workload you want to carry.
- How well you know your own finances.
- How well you know the markets.
- How much control you want over your investments.

By and large, the personal portfolio investor is already savvy in the ways of Wall Street, has bought and sold stocks before, or has good experience investing in mutual funds.

That said, he's no Warren Buffett. So the early argument for a folio investor having access to a financial advisor, as I mentioned, is to save him from himself. So says Gavin Quill, senior vice president of FRC Monitor, an investment trends publication. In an interview that appeared on the Web site Forum for Investor Advice *(www.investoradvice.org)*, Quill makes the following argument for having a financial advisor. "Traditionally, investors could put their money in one, individual stocks and bonds or two, pooled vehicles, primarily mutual funds," he says. "Recently, however, a number of 'third way' investment products have emerged to broaden the number of choices. These alternative products range from old-line vehicles now made more widely available, such as private investment accounts, to totally new concepts, such as 'stock baskets,' better known as 'folios.'

"There are two trends here," he continues. "The first is that you will always have the direct, Web-savvy investors who are early adopters. They're the one percent who are ahead of every curve. The smart broker and planner lets them go out and kick the tires.

"Then brokers and planners bring new products into the mainstream. They're far better at integrating them into an investor's portfolio without disruption than the direct investor. The direct investor is likely to do something foolish, such as selling a portion of his portfolio in order to try a new product, but then realizing too late that there are negative tax consequences in what he's done."

Quill adds that the role of the financial advisor in the personal portfolio process is to help investors make fewer emotional decisions. "Our research shows that investors typically trade way too much, and at the wrong time," he says. Why? Because they're emotionally wedded to their assets—it's human nature. Advisors help investors with three important steps: gaining market knowledge, gaining self knowledge, and providing the will to implement decisions—pulling the lever when it's time, and not pulling it when it's not time.

Granted, that outlook sort of flies in the face of the notion that nobody is more qualified to manage your money than you are. Hey, Suze Orman's made a fortune convincing investors that going solo is the way to go when it comes to money management.

But perhaps a combination—or an investor/mentor relationship—may actually work for you when you're managing your own portfolio. At the least, you're still making the final investment decisions but a financial advisor is acting as a sounding board and giving you a professional second opinion.

Going Halfway

One idea is to take the "half a loaf" approach on the financial advisor question. Instead of shelling out thousands of dollars for a financial advisor to take over all of your money management responsibilities, why not opt for a lesser approach and take on a financial advisor on a part-time basis? At companies like Garrett Planning Network *(www.garrettplanningnetwork. com),* you can log on and ask for financial advice on your personal portfolio on an hourly basis.

Here's how it works. Instead of laying out something like $3,000 annually for a full-time advisor, Garrett Networks has a fully accredited financial advisory staff on hand to take your calls and questions for an average of $125 per hour.

Say, for example, you've read this book and checked out some personal portfolio packages. You sign up for one, do your risk and asset allocation profiles, and start the process of picking stocks. How could it hurt to show an advisor at a company like Garret Networks the portfolio you have in mind? Chances are you could wrap the whole thing up in one or two hours and you've only paid $150 or so. Periodically, say every time you change your portfolio, or once or twice a year, you could call the advisor back with a question or two on issues like rebalancing and taxes. Total cost to you for the year would still be well under $1,000.

Or, if you prefer working from your computer and are comfortable using financial software, a number of personal financial advisory Web sites exist that offer you software programs to evaluate your portfolio choices and deliver some good investment advice on issues like stock selection, risk and diversification, and asset allocation. Try Financial Engines *(www.financialengines.com)* or Charles Schwab *(www.schwab.com)*. Both offer similar services and, if you have a good handle on your investments, probably provide the best bang for your financial advisory buck.

Common Mistakes You Can Make Without a Financial Advisor

Here's an informal list of mistakes investors can make by not using a financial advisor. See if any apply to you:

Getting emotional about your investments—Nobody likes to admit they made a mistake. So who's to know if that bow-wow of a stock you bought at $30 and has since fallen to $5 is swept under the rug? Or who's to argue that it won't bounce back? I hate to keep picking on the Enron shareholders, but that's exactly what happened to them. First, they watched in disbelief as the stocks began sinking. Then they engaged in a fatal case of wishful thinking by agreeing with those despicable company executives who placated investors by saying the company would weather the storm and rally the stock to new heights. Then the skunks upstairs went out and began dumping their own shares like crazy.

Picking the wrong asset allocation mix—As I mentioned before, it's much worse getting the allocation wrong than it is getting the stock picking wrong. As long as you've honed in on the correct asset class, like large-cap stocks or Treasury bonds, then you're 90 percent of the way home, as the historical evidence suggests. But if you pick the wrong asset class—see the oil industry in 1990 or small-cap growth stocks in 2000 for proof—you're really up against it.

Remaining on the sidelines when you need to be in the game—Things happen over the course of your life. People get married, get divorced, buy and sell houses, take and lose jobs. All of these events trigger equally significant financial shock waves that need to be dealt with. But too often people don't act when they should and wind up all the poorer because the financial framework they've established for themselves is old and creaky and inadequate for all the changes that have taken place in their lives.

Failing to take the future into account—Half of financial planning is preparing for what will happen to you down the road. When do you want to retire? When are your kids going to college? When do you want to start that new freelance graphic design business you've always wanted? If you build a personal portfolio around your present financial circumstances and disregard your future financial circumstances, you're only decreasing your chances of meeting those future goals.

Again, a sharp financial advisor can help you avoid these pitfalls.

Types of Financial Advisors

When I toss around the term "financial advisors," just who am I talking about? Good question. Financial advisors come in a mix of categories and expertise. Some specialize in portfolio management. Some are tax experts. Some are more proficient in estate planning and other legal areas. The one thing they all have in common is that financial advisors must pass a rigorous testing process to hang their shingle and go into business as financial planners. That means they are registered in your state to do business as financial advisors.

Let's look at the primary categories of the advisors who've earned the right to call themselves financial experts.

- **Certified Financial Planners (CFPs)**—have completed a two-year course and have passed tough exams with the

College for Financial Planning or the Certified Financial Planner Board of Standards. They can offer tax planning, estate planning, portfolio management, and insurance advising. While some planners earn all their income from commissions, others charge a fee, which can range from $50 to $200 an hour.

• **Chartered Financial Consultants/Chartered Life Underwriters (ChFCs/CLUs)**—have finished a three-year course with the American College located in Bryn Mawr, Pennsylvania, near Philadelphia. They can offer services in tax, estate, insurance, financial, and investment management. Insurance agents (or life underwriters) are licensed by the state.

• **Certified Public Accountants (CPAs)**—often offer financial services that go beyond tax accounting. CPAs who have passed their Personal Financial Specialist exams have at least 250 hours of yearly experience in financial planning.

• **Certified Consumer Credit Counselors (CCCCs)**—are certified by the National Foundation for Consumer Credit and offer assistance with budgeting and basic money management, as well as advice on how to get out of debt and how to use credit wisely. If your needs are basic, a credit counselor can be a smart choice, since many offer their services free of charge through a Consumer Credit Counseling Service agency.

• **Registered Representatives (also known as Registered Financial Consultants [RFC])**—also known more informally as stockbrokers, registered reps buy and sell securities on behalf of their clients for a commission. Many financial planners are also brokers for one or more investment firms and earn a commission on the sale of investment products.

For more information on the different types of financial advisors and which ones might be right for you, contact the North American Securities Administrators Association at 202-737-0900.

Where to Find a Financial Advisor?

Most people find their financial advisors in one of two ways: either through a referral from a friend, relative, or business associate; or through the Yellow Pages or somewhere on the World Wide Web.

There's a third way that few people consider—by going directly to the associations that accredit financial planners. Here is a list of the main financial advisory trade associations. Contact them directly and they'll either recommend or send you a list of suitable financial advisors in your area.

Financial Planning Association
800-322-4237
www.fpanet.org

National Association of Personal Financial Advisors
Suite 200, 355 W. Dundee Road
Buffalo Grove, IL 60089
800-FEE-ONLY
www.napfa.org

American Institute of Certified Public Accountants
Personal Financial Planning Division
Harborside Financial Center
201 Plaza 3
Jersey City, NJ 07311-3881
888-777-7077
www.aicpa.org

American Society of Financial Service Professionals
Consumer Referral Service
270 S. Bryn Mawr Avenue
Bryn Mawr, PA 19010
800-392-6900
www.financialpro.org

International Association of Registered Financial Consultants
The Financial Planning Building
P.O. Box 42506
Middletown, OH 45042
800-532-9060
www.iarfc.org

Know Beforehand What You Want Your Financial Advisor to Do

When you begin the process of winnowing your financial advisor candidates down to size, make a list of the qualities you want in a financial advisor and the things you expect them to do for you. That way you won't have any misunderstandings later on about who's doing what for whom. The list will also give you a nice blueprint to work from when you're meeting with individual financial advisors you're thinking of hiring.

The list should include how the advisor will be paid. Advisors are usually paid one of three ways:

1. On a commission basis—Most planners work under this arrangement. Say, for example, you're going to invest $30,000 in your personal portfolio. If your advisor charges a commission of 5 percent, then the advisor will take the 5 percent—$1,500—right off the top and invest the rest.

2. On an hourly basis—Financial planners can charge up to $300 per hour. Most, though, settle into the $100–$200 category.

3. On a "fee" basis—Financial planners who charge on a fee basis will establish a figure right up front of what they're going to charge you for the services they provide. For example, if you engage a financial planner to create your entire personal portfolio from scratch she may charge you, say, $10,000 for everything. But if she is just going to review your

portfolio and make sure it meets your financial goals she may only charge you $500 or $1,000 per year to do so. A note on fee-only planners: Since they don't get paid on commission there's no perceived "conflict of interest" of recommending stocks for your personal portfolio that earns them a commission. I'm not saying that such conflicts happen all the time—but they do happen.

Get a Written Agreement

When you decide on a financial advisor make sure you get a written agreement from him spelling out in exact terms the services he will provide and the fees he will charge you. Read it thoroughly before signing it. If you have access to a lawyer, have her read it, too.

Ask for Form ADV

Form ADV is the document that discloses any potential trouble spots or conflicts of interest on the part of your financial advisor. It's also a good idea to call the financial planning organization the advisor is affiliated with and check to see if there are any complaints or lawsuits against that advisor.

Get an Investment Policy Statement Up Front

An investor policy statement is a document signed by both you and your advisor spelling out the investment strategy you've decided to pursue. Having that strategy down on paper can save you a lot of problems later on if your personal portfolio program goes off the beam and both you and your financial advisor begin pointing fingers. Specifics to include in the statement are: target return, risk tolerance, time horizon, and tax liability issues.

Questions to Ask a Financial Advisor

Hiring a financial planner is not much different than hiring a doctor, a carpenter, or a real estate agent to sell your home.

You have to ask a lot of questions to get a sense of how compatible you are with your advisor.

While most advisors will provide you with a brochure or kit detailing their background, qualifications, services, compensation structure, business partnerships, hours of operation, reporting methods, and preferred modes of communication, you have to dig a little deeper to find out exactly if an advisor is right for you.

But what questions to ask? Here are some that should provide you with a good idea of how effective your advisor will be working for you:

1. Are you accredited as a licensed financial advisor? If not, sorry. Only qualified applicants need apply.

2. Have you ever been sued by a client? Do you have a history of complaints from clients? You'll probably need to get this information yourself from one of the financial planning associations that track such things. But ask a potential advisor anyway and watch closely as she answers. Any hesitation or apparent nervousness may be a red flag.

3. How are you paid? Fee-only planners are probably your best bet. That way you're getting objective investment advice and there's no conflict of interest from having to pay commissions on stocks you bought with your advisor's say so.

4. Could I see your form ADV? It's another red flag if the advisor can't produce a form ADV. Most states require advisors to have them.

5. What's your background? I hate to stereotype, but given a choice between an advisor who has a master's degree from Wharton and who spent five years on a Wall Street trading desk or a guy who only last year was selling multilevel marketing programs, I'd go with the former over the latter. After all, you don't want to be an advisor's first client. Let them learn their mistakes with someone else's money.

6. How many clients do you have? Can I talk to them? I like financial advisors with a small regional base of clients.

The larger firms that have a national presence may not give you the personal "face time" care and management that you need. I'm not saying all the big firms are like that, but isn't it better if you can just walk in off the street and say "hello" to your advisor? I think so. In addition, a good financial advisor will happily provide you with the phone number of a client or two who can vouch for his character, qualifications, and effectiveness. If they balk—take a walk.

7.   What's your investment style? A big question. Some financial advisors are specialists in one area and some are specialists in another. You might find an advisor who insists that technology stocks have no place in a portfolio. You might find another advisor who favors small growth companies as investment vehicles. Some advisors advocate marketing timing. Others tout buy-and-hold strategies. Who's right? Who knows? Just make sure that you and your advisor share some common ground on what types of investment strategies work for you. One other point: Make sure your investment advisor can explain his or her investment philosophy in the time it takes to boil an egg. Leave the longwinded types to other investors. You want sound, basic, easy-to-understand advice.

8.   What does your portfolio look like? Knowing what your advisor invests his or her money in provides a glimpse into his or her personal philosophies on investing. That's not to say that what is right for your advisor is right for you. But a lot can be discerned from the investing practices of the financial professional you're about to hire.

What You Need to Tell Your Financial Advisor

Prior to the hiring of a financial advisor, you'll be asking all the questions. But after the advisor is on board, it's your turn to start answering some questions.

Relax, it's not one of those hokey police shows where grim-faced detectives lock you in a hot room for hours with a lone light bulb swinging over your head. In fact, answering some questions from an investment professional is a good exercise for you. A little Q & A helps you verbalize your investment ideals and allows you to lay out your portfolio game plan.

What questions will your advisor ask? Fairly basic ones, along the lines of "Where are you financially?" or "What are your financial goals?" Your advisor will want a full account of your tolerance for risk and how involved you want to be in your investment decisions. Since you're building your own personal portfolio, of course you'll answer "very involved" to that query.

One last note: A relationship between an investor and a financial advisor is akin to being married, with your portfolio being your "child." You're going to have your ups and downs and you're certainly not going to agree on everything. It's hard working with someone else when your money is involved, but try to remember that your financial advisor is professionally trained to help you make more, not less, money. A good advisor always has your best interests in mind and won't steer you down a path you don't want to go.

My take on the personal portfolio/advisor issue? I'd get one—at least part-time. It's always good to have a sounding board from an objective source who has your best interests in mind.

Happy hunting.

Case Study: *Getting Another Opinion*

Joan Donaldson was fully confident she could build her own personal portfolio. But she had to admit that, deep down inside, she would feel a lot better if she could show her portfolio to a financial professional. She'd feel even better knowing she could pick up a phone once in a while and ask a financial pro an investment question or two.

"I'm fairly independent," says the fifty-nine-year-old retiree. "I had a great career as a working woman and made a lot of money. But having taken my retirement distributions in a lump sum payment, I knew I couldn't just let it sit there. I wanted to invest it and I wanted to do as much of it myself as I could."

Joan opened an account with a personal portfolio company and began researching the types of stocks and bonds she wanted to include in her fund. "I wanted stability, first and foremost," she says. "I've accumulated a great deal of money over the years and now I have to think about preserving it."

That said, she knew that with her family's history of living well into their nineties, she'd need to take some risk.

"I decided to enlist the help of a financial advisor to help me come up with the right asset allocation mix for my portfolio," she says. "I interviewed a few advisors until I met the one who made the most sense for me."

Clinching the deal was the advisor's penchant for logical, sound reasoning for buying a stock. "Offhandedly, I'd mentioned to him that there was this speculative stock I was thinking of buying," she says. "He said, 'O.K.—but you're not buying it through me.' That showed me he was looking out for my best interests."

Joan Donaldson Personal Portfolio
ALLOCATION PERCENTAGES
30% aggressive growth stocks
30% value stocks
10% large-cap growth stocks
20% corporate bonds
10% cash
FOLIO FAVORITES
Wal-Mart, U.S. Bancorp, Con Edison

Chapter Checklist

✓ At first glance, hiring a financial advisor to help you manage your personal portfolio seems to run counter to the whole idea of running your own fund. But on further review, it helps to have some objective advice when you're building your fund.

✓ You don't have to hire a full-time investment advisor. Pay by the hour and hire a part-time advisor. Then go ahead and build your fund on your own—just run it by your advisor before you actually start making any trades.

✓ Make sure your financial advisor is fully accredited and licensed by your state. Qualified advisors have to pass some rigorous tests before they can practice as financial advisors.

✓ Get an ADV form from a potential advisor. It's a form that tells you whether the advisor has been in hot water with other clients before.

✓ Ask a lot of questions. How is the advisor paid? What does he or she invest in? What's his or her background? Treat the financial advisory process as you would the process of hiring a nanny or a family doctor. The more you know now—the fewer surprises there may be later on.

Chapter 10

Doing Well by Doing Good: Socially Responsible Investing

*"We make a living by what we get.
We make a life by what we give."*
—ANONYMOUS

ollywood legend has it that legendary producer Louis B. Mayer was asked to make a donation to charity. He said "No." Rebuffed, the person told Mayer that, when it comes to money, "You can't take it with you." Unmoved, Mayer quickly replied, "Then I won't go."

Like many funny anecdotes the Mayer story has a dark side—his inability to part with his money runs so deep that he'll cheat death rather than write a check to charity. Some people, for whatever reason, live their lives under the credo "what's mine is mine and what's yours is yours." The fact that they have more than the other guy usually goes unmentioned.

Fortunately, the vast majority of Americans don't feel this way. Statistically, we're far and away the leading country in charitable donations. According to the nonprofit group the American Association of Fundraising Counsel (AAFRC) Trust for Philanthropy, Americans gave an estimated $212 billion to charity in 2001, a year in which recession and terrorism hampered economic and investment growth.

"Americans' commitment to philanthropy remained strong even in the face of downward economic pressures," said John J. Glier, chairman of the AAFRC. "The $212 billion total is the highest level of giving ever reported."

Individual Americans were far and away the largest providers of charitable wealth. Again, according to the AAFRC, individual donors gave an estimated $160.72 billion to charity, representing 75.8 percent of all giving estimated for 2001. Compare that to corporate giving, which fell way back to $9 billion, comprising 12 percent of all charitable donations.

Giving When It Hurts

What's more, Americans really begin to dig deep and give charitably when things are at their worst.

According to a study by the Center of Philanthropy at Indiana University that looked at charitable trends in the immediate aftermath of catastrophic national events, like Pearl Harbor and the Cuban Missile Crisis, Americans continued to give vast sums of money to charitable organizations. They did so even though in the vast majority of instances the stock market had dropped conspicuously immediately after these events and the economy often careened out of control.

"We know that giving is closely correlated with the economy, and there do seem to be some fairly consistent trends in giving and in the economy in the years surrounding these major national events," said Patrick M. Rooney, director of research and chief operating officer for the Center on Philanthropy.

In fact, the total amount of charitable giving in the United States has increased every year but one (1987) for the past forty years, despite wars, recessions, and other crises. Although the rate of growth has varied from year to year, each year Americans have given more than the previous year.

"Our findings from this evaluation and other studies show that both the stock market and giving are resilient," said Eugene R. Tempel, executive director of the Center on Philanthropy. "While this is a unique situation, in the past Americans have shown a remarkable capacity to recover from adversity, both economically and spiritually, as measured by the stock market and giving."

Investing and Social Responsibility

Okay, so we've determined that, when it comes to charitable giving, even in times of economic and political peril, nobody beats the American public.

But how does that impulse to give and do well translate into your personal portfolio? Easy. Cultural observers like the AAFRC are on to something. They see that Americans not only want to accumulate wealth, but they also want to share some of that wealth. The charitable giving story is just the most obvious and most prominent example of that trend. But there are other factors at work, too, when it comes to Americans and their money. Not only do they not mind giving money away, but they're also developing an appetite for investing in companies that satisfy their ethical needs *and* that meet their high standards for good corporate citizenship.

In recent years, this trend has manifested itself in what's come to be known as socially responsible investing. I'll get to what that means in a moment. Within the confines of this book, what matters is that there is no better way to invest in socially responsible companies than through personal portfolios.

First, the skinny on socially responsible investments.

Purse Power

Women account for just 48 percent of mutual-fund shareholders, but they make up about 60 percent of all socially conscious investors, reports the Social Investment Forum (www.socialinvest.org), a nonprofit group promoting socially responsible investing. While men make up an estimated 90 percent of the leadership of mutual funds, it's women who dominate the top positions at socially responsible funds. ❖

What Is Socially Responsible Investing?

Socially responsible investing is the natural extension of charitable giving. Through socially responsible investing, Americans can—and often do—opt to invest in companies that meet their ethical standards.

Whether that means avoiding companies that produce pollution or make alcohol, or latching onto companies that promote alternative energy sources, social responsibility is one of the hottest trends in global investing.

Socially responsible investing traces its origins back to biblical times when Jewish merchants agreed to abide by commonly approved ethical standards when conducting business. In the United States, the Quakers have a long tradition of demonstrating socially conscious business practices that dates back to their arrival on American shores in the early 1600s. By and large, however, socially conscious investing took a back seat to the business of making money over the ensuing centuries. In fact, it wasn't until the 1970s when socially responsible investing heated up with sanctions against the government of South Africa. The government there practiced apartheid—institutionalized racial discrimination—and was ultimately held accountable by outraged global consumers and investors, many of whom vowed never to invest a nickel in the South African economy until blacks were treated with more respect and given equal legal status.

Contributing to the rise of socially responsible investing during this time was the American civil rights struggle. Companies that set up shop in poor minority communities and proved to be indifferent corporate neighbors soon found themselves the target of mass protests and boycotts. The same thing happened on a global stage. Companies like Nike, Kmart, and others who, fairly or unfairly, were accused by activists of running sweatshops and underpaying workers were dragged under the harsh glare of the ethical spotlight. In the 1980s, as investors enjoyed a rise in worldwide capital markets with big gains in global stock exchanges, organizations like the Interfaith Center for Corporate Responsibility (ICCR) and the Social Investment Forum began popping up to shape public policy on corporate standards and began tracking companies they considered to be off the beam, ethics-wise.

By the '80s, activists had found socially responsible investing to be a useful tool against corporate malfeasance. Witness the backlash against Exxon when the oil tanker *Valdez* sank in Alaska's Prince William Sound, releasing millions of gallons of oil into the bay. When Exxon initially refused to come clean, activists rallied investors and held the company accountable. Nowadays it's common practice for investors to think twice before investing in companies that have blemished records on issues like toxic waste or global warming, or have lackluster human rights policies in their operations.

Here's some indications of how rapidly this phenomenon of socially responsible investing has grown. In 1999, $1 out of every $8 invested in stocks was prompted by a socially conscious decision. That comes to $2.16 trillion of the $16.3 trillion professionally managed in the United States, or 13 percent. The $2.16 trillion figure is up 82 percent from 1997. And back in 1984, there were only $40 billion in socially responsible investing.

Socially Responsible Investors Make an Impact

If you want proof that socially responsible investing is for real, just ask the management at Home Depot, the do-it-yourself retail giant. In 1999, the company was forced by activist investors to stop the sale of old-growth wood products—wood from forests that had never been logged—at a shareholder meeting in Atlanta. Pressured by environmental groups who picketed the meeting and lobbied aggressively by "green" groups like Rainforest Action, 11 percent of shareholders voted to stop the practice. That got the ball rolling.

Protesters began picketing Home Depot stores where activists with bullhorns shouted "Attention shoppers, there's a special in aisle 23 on products made from old-growth timber." By 2000, backed by the votes of 4,000 shareholders and 150 institutional investors, the activists won out and the store stopped the practice of using old-wood products. Soon, competitors like Lowes and Sears followed suit. Environmentalists called it one of the greatest victories ever.

Home Depot is hardly alone. In past years other companies have felt the sting of investor activism, including:

- **Sara Lee**—The company sold its Drum rolling tobacco business, which had generated $300 million in annual sales.
- **Atlantic Richfield, Texaco, and Pepsico**—All three companies left Burma because of the military dictatorship's denial of human rights and democracy.
- **RJR Nabisco**—Remember Joe Camel? The consumer goods giant made millions from its Joe Camel advertising, especially in sales of cigarettes to teens. In 1988, the year Joe Camel was introduced, cigarette sales to teens amounted to $6 million. By 1992, that number had grown to $476 million. Still, activist investors forced Joe Camel back into hiding.
- **McDonald's**—In 1999 the fast-food giant added sexual orientation to its nondiscrimination statement after intense lobbying from Trillium Asset Management, a major institutional investor. Trillium was also among the first institutional investors to file a resolution on sweatshops, persuading Wal-Mart to adopt guidelines for vendors that barred the use of child labor.
- **General Electric**—The company promoted a woman into senior management for the first time, after pressure from a major investor, Aquinas Funds in Dallas, Texas. GE also agreed to spend $250 million to clean up a river in western Massachusetts that activists claim was polluted by the company's nearby manufacturing plant.

- **Ford Motor Company**—The automaker resigned from the controversial Global Climate Coalition—a group of companies that promotes doubts about global warming—following pressure from the Interfaith Center on Corporate Responsibility (ICCR) in New York City.
- **Baxter International**—After sustained pressure from shareholders, the world's largest health-care products manufacturer began to phase out polyvinyl chloride (PVC) materials in its intravenous products.
- **RJ Reynolds**—Shareholders forced the consumer giant to split its tobacco business from its food business.

These examples are only the tip of the iceberg. It's a rare company that doesn't take its corporate image into account when it courts shareholders. Crafting a caring, community-oriented corporate persona isn't a luxury these days, particularly in light of recent ethical disasters in corporate America, it's a necessity.

Social Responsibility and Investor Demand

Apparently, investors like what they see from socially responsible companies. According to Financial Research Corp., investors plowed $1.3 billion of new money into socially responsible funds during the first half of 2002, compared to $847 million added during all of 2001.❖

Socially Responsible Investing and Folios

For years mutual funds were the prime beneficiaries of socially conscious investors. Fund firms like Calvert Group and Citizens Funds have built entire operations around the marketing of various (what the industry has come to call) "SRI" funds. There's little doubt that socially responsible investors came to rely on these mutual funds. The number of socially responsible mutual funds using one or more social criteria has grown to nearly 200 funds and includes equity, balanced, international, bond, index, and money market funds.

Overall, $13 billion has been directly invested in SRI funds, according to Morningstar Research; this makes up about 2 percent of overall mutual fund assets through 2002. Overall, assets invested in socially responsible investments worldwide (including funds, personal portfolios, and separately managed accounts) is about $2 trillion, according to Calvert Group.

Another, more recent reason for the growth in the SRI sector is the corporate scandals of the early 2000s. With companies like Arthur Anderson and Tyco drowning in their own malfeasance, investors grew disgusted with corporate greed and began looking more closely at firms that had higher ethical standards and played by the rules. Socially responsible funds saw their inflows rise in 2002, the flashpoint of the corporate accountability scandals. Conversely, conventional funds saw their coffers drained during the same period. "If we're going to lose our money," people seemed to be saying, "let's at least lose it while doing the right thing."

Other reasons account for the popularity of SRI. With the advent of the Internet and its army of do-it-yourselfers who could cruise the Web and research their own socially responsible companies, the need to pay a mutual fund an exorbitant fee and place themselves in a potentially disadvantageous tax situation led investors to alternative investment tools like the personal portfolio.

Enter folio firms like FOLIO*fn* and E*Trade, which have no shortage of SRI options for the discriminating investor. Unlike the mutual fund world, where investors have no control over the companies that comprise their funds, personal portfolios enable investors to create their own diverse portfolios of socially responsible stocks. With personal portfolios, investors can customize holdings to keep an arm's length from companies and industries they disapprove of, like tobacco stocks or drug companies engaged in animal testing.

Say you want to build a large-cap portfolio that's heavy on the consumer goods side. With a mutual fund, you might have to take a tobacco company or two, or absorb a company with a weak record on the environment. In the fund world it's an "all or nothing" mentality that leaves little room for ethical standards and investor flexibility.

With a personal portfolio, you can build that large-cap fund and leave Phillip Morris or RJR Nabisco out of it. How do you do that? Two ways, actually. First, a good folio company will do the screening for you. They'll either have a menu of SRI folios all ready to go. All you have to do is to pick the one you like. See the sample folios below from FOLIO*fn*:

Sample Tobacco-Free Folio from FOLIOfn

#	SYMBOL	COMPANY	WEIGHT (% OF FOLIO)
1.	ABT	ABBOTT LABS	3.33%
2.	AIG	AMERICAN INTL GROUP INC	3.33%
3.	AMGN	AMGEN INC	3.33%
4.	BAC	BANK OF AMERICA CORPORATION	3.33%
5.	C	CITIGROUP INC	3.33%
6.	CSCO	CISCO SYS INC	3.34%
7.	CVX	CHEVRONTEXACO CORP	3.33%
8.	DELL	DELL COMPUTER CORP	3.33%
9.	FNM	FEDERAL NATL MTG ASSN	3.33%
10.	GE	GENERAL ELEC CO	3.33%
11.	HD	HOME DEPOT INC	3.33%
12.	IBM	INTERNATIONAL BUSINESS MACHS	3.33%
13.	INTC	INTEL CORP	3.33%
14.	JNJ	JOHNSON & JOHNSON	3.33%
15.	KO	COCA COLA CO	3.33%
16.	LLY	LILLY ELI & CO	3.33%
17.	MDT	MEDTRONIC INC	3.33%

Sample Tobacco-Free Folio from FOLIOfn (continued)

#	Symbol	Company	Weight (% of Folio)
18.	MRK	MERCK & CO INC	3.33%
19.	MSFT	MICROSOFT CORP	3.33%
20.	PEP	PEPSICO INC	3.33%
21.	PFE	PFIZER INC	3.33%
22.	PG	PROCTER & GAMBLE CO	3.33%
23.	PHA	PHARMACIA CORP	3.33%
24.	SBC	SBC COMMUNICATIONS INC	3.33%
25.	UPS	UNITED PARCEL SERVICE INC CL B	3.33%
26.	VIA	VIACOM INC CL A	3.33%
27.	VZ	VERIZON COMMUNICATIONS INC.	3.33%
28.	WFC	WELLS FARGO & CO NEW	3.33%
29.	WMT	WAL-MART STORES INC	3.33%
30.	XOM	EXXON MOBIL CORP	3.33%

Source: FOLIOfn.

But you can also customize and build your own socially responsible personal portfolios and do the screening yourself. Building an SRI portfolio is no different than building a basic personal portfolio. You have to consider your financial objectives and your social objectives and find a way to accommodate both of them.

The first thing to do is to decide what your social priorities are. Are you an avid eco-environmentalist? An enthusiastic opponent of tobacco and pro-tobacco industry legislation? Or maybe you're a proud multiculturist who refuses to invest in companies with lax diversity practices. Construct your portfolio around your decisions.

How Far Should You Go?

The next move to make is to figure out how far you want to go in punishing companies that don't meet your ethical standards. For instance, rejecting Phillip Morris would seem to be a natural notion to a reformed antismoker. But what about the companies that make the boxes that the company uses for its cigarettes? Or how about the publishing companies in whose magazines the ads for Phillip Morris appear? Should you avoid them, too?

That's the direct/indirect dilemma. At first blush, it might be easier to avoid the companies that sell products you don't agree with first and worry about the companies that do business with those companies later—if at all.

Then apply the same criteria you would in building your regular investment portfolio. Consider your risk comfort level, your current financial picture, your future financial needs, and your need to diversify among different investments. For example, it's great to include a company or two that specializes in solar energy. But you wouldn't want fifteen or twenty such companies in your folio. If you do that, you'll surely get burned.

The next step is to conduct research on the companies in the SRI sectors you favor. Use the same strategies we discussed in Chapter 7—read the company prospectus, research the company on the Web, using Google.com and/or Hoovers.com, specifically. Take a look at company financials, including earning and sales figures. Check out management, too. Some eco-environmental companies are so brand-new that management hasn't had much experience in running a business. Sounds cold, I know. But socially responsible or not, it's still your money we're talking about. In fact, that should be the foremost thing in your mind when investing in socially responsible companies. By all means, do the right thing and invest where your heart lies. But don't leave your head out of the equation, either.

When you begin picking stocks for your SRI folio, try to factor in the attempts companies are making to do social good. Take the pharmaceutical industry. Yes, it's widely known (among environmental activists, at least) that the industry has a poor track record on pollution. But when you look closer, you see companies like Johnson & Johnson and Merck & Company that have installed strong antipollution measures in their operations that go above and beyond what Uncle Sam says they have to do. Other companies in the industry have not done that. That's why stock picking in the SRI sector is so nuanced. No company—even in the same industry—is behaving exactly like another company. They're all different.

Also, pay attention to corporate subsidiaries. At first glance, you may not find anything wrong investing in Hartmann luggage or Lenox china. But, if you're a teetotaler who abhors investing your money in alcohol companies, you might not realize that the company that owns Hartmann and Lenox is Brown-Forman, makers of Jack Daniels bourbon.

Getting Help Building a Socially Responsible Folio

Since screening for socially responsible companies is tougher than researching companies based on financial considerations alone, it's a good idea to get some help. Fortunately, there's no shortage of SRI watchdog groups available to lend a helping hand to your due diligence needs. SocialFunds.com (*www.socialfunds.com*), for example, provides data on 2,000 large and mid-size companies. They'll also list specific products—like alcohol, tobacco, firearms—that specific companies sell. They'll also detail how many workers have been killed or injured in industrial accidents and rank companies in areas like toxic emissions and diversity hiring practices. A note: Such companies are under no formal restrictions from the government on what they can or cannot say. Consequently, there's some room for stretching the truth.

Here's a quick look at other companies to turn to for help in identifying the correct socially conscious companies for your personal portfolio.

- CSRwire.com—Gives SRI investors a menu of 600 companies that impact key issues like eco-environment and human rights. Companies covered include: Intel, IBM, and McDonald's. The site will tell you, for example, that McDonald's makes 40 percent of its cartons, paper bags, and boxes from recycled material.
- Crosswalk.com—Provides "value reports," based on fundamentalist Christian beliefs that criticize companies for producing antifamily entertainment and other activities.
- TheMotleyFool.com—Provides a socially responsible investing discussion board.
- CorporateRegister.com—Offers detailed information on the hiring and management practices of U.S. companies.

A Sample Environment Friendly Portfolio from FOLIOfn

#	Symbol	Company	Weight (% of Folio)
1.	AIG	AMERICAN INTL GROUP INC	3.33%
2.	AMGN	AMGEN INC	3.33%
3.	BAC	BANK OF AMERICA CORPORATION	3.33%
4.	CCU	CLEAR CHANNEL COMMUNICATIONS	3.33%
5.	CSCO	CISCO SYS INC	3.33%
6.	DELL	DELL COMPUTER CORP	3.33%
7.	FBF	FLEETBOSTON FINL CORP	3.33%
8.	FDC	FIRST DATA CORP	3.33%
9.	FITB	FIFTH THIRD BANCORP	3.33%
10.	FNM	FEDERAL NATL MTG ASSN	3.33%
11.	FRE	FEDERAL HOME LN MTG CORP	3.33%
12.	GS	GOLDMAN SACHS GROUP INC	3.33%
13.	HCA	HCA-HEALTHCARE COMPANY	3.33%
14.	JPM	J P MORGAN CHASE & CO	3.34%
15.	KRB	MBNA CORP	3.33%
16.	LOW	LOWES COS INC	3.33%
17.	MDT	MEDTRONIC INC	3.33%

A Sample Environment Friendly Portfolio from FOLIOfn (cont'd)

#	SYMBOL	COMPANY	WEIGHT (% OF FOLIO)
18.	MMC	MARSH & MCLENNAN COS INC	3.33%
19.	MSFT	MICROSOFT CORP	3.33%
20.	MWD	MORGAN STANLEY DEAN WITTER & CO NEW	3.33%
21.	ONE	BANK ONE CORP	3.33%
22.	ORCL	ORACLE CORP	3.33%
23.	QCOM	QUALCOMM INC	3.33%
24.	THC	TENET HEALTHCARE CORP	3.33%
25.	UNH	UNITEDHEALTH GROUP	3.33%
26.	USB	US BANCORP DEL	3.33%
27.	WB	WACHOVIA CORP 2ND NEW	3.33%
28.	WFC	WELLS FARGO & CO NEW	3.33%
29.	WM	WASHINGTON MUT INC	3.33%
30.	WMT	WAL-MART STORES INC	3.33%

Source: FOLIOfn.

Socially Responsible Investing and Market Performance

You'd think that avoiding companies that sold big money-making products like cigarettes or alcohol would be a huge mistake from an investing point of view. But it's not.

In fact, a recent report by Mellon Equity Associates said that the avoidance of tobacco companies in an SRI portfolio need not result in underperformance. Other, more appropriate stocks with better financial characteristics are often substituted, and/or the tobacco industry could simply be avoided altogether with no attempt to replace it. Another study by Kinder, Lyndenberg & Domini discovered that many mutual funds that refused to invest in tobacco actually outperformed the market. What's more, the Domini 400 SRI Index, which has never included tobacco companies, has always beaten the S&P 500 Index since its inception in May of 1990.

In fact, the Domini 400 Index—an index comprised of prescreened socially responsible companies has outperformed the S&P Index for ten years through 2002, by more than 2 percentage points per year.

"It's no wonder socially oriented investments are growing twice as fast as other investments," said Marjorie Kelly, publisher of *Business Ethics*, a thirteen-year-old publication on corporate social responsibility. "Socially sensitive management is simply a better way to manage."

Socially Responsible Investing Edges Out S&P 500

The Domini 400 SocialSM Index (DSI) is the established benchmark for measuring the impact of social screening on financial performance. Launched in May 1990, the DSI is the first benchmark for equity portfolios subject to multiple social screens.

The DSI has outperformed the S&P 500 on a total return basis and on a risk-adjusted basis since its inception in May 1990. The table shows the comparative total return performance of the DSI and the S&P 500.

KLD publishes the Statistical Review of the DSI each month. It contains performance data, financial statistics, and listings of companies in the index. Here is some information on the performance and makeup of the Domini index:

DSI Performance Statistics

TOTAL RETURN AS OF 12/31/02	*DSI 400*	*S&P 500*
December 2002	-6.37%	-5.86%
YTD	-20.10%	-22.09%
Last Qtr	9.25%	8.46%
One Year	-20.10%	-22.09%
Three Year *	-15.57%	-14.52%
Five Year *	0.17%	-0.55%
Ten Year *	9.99%	9.35%

* Annualized Returns

DSI Top 10 Holdings (09/30/02)

Cisco Systems, Inc.

Wells Fargo & Company

Intel Corporation

Bank of America Corporation

Merck & Company, Inc.

Procter & Gamble Company

Coca-Cola Company

American International
Group, Inc.

Johnson & Johnson

Microsoft Corporation

Source: Domini 400 Social Index.

Here is an example of a portfolio compiled by FOLIO*fn* focusing on companies with strong female leadership:

"Women Leaders" Portfolio (Firms with High Numbers of Female Executives) from FOLIOfn

#	SYMBOL	COMPANY	WEIGHT (% OF FOLIO)
1.	ADPT	ADAPTEC INC	4.17%
2.	AET	AETNA INC NEW COM	3.20%
3.	AVID	AVID TECHNOLOGY INC	3.20%
4.	AVP	AVON PRODS INC	5.83%
5.	AWR	AMERICAN STS WTR CO	2.82%
6.	BCC	BOISE CASCADE CORP	2.82%
7.	CHS	CHICOS FAS INC	3.20%
8.	CL	COLGATE PALMOLIVE CO	2.82%
9.	CLE	CLAIRES STORES INC	2.82%
10.	EBAY	EBAY INC	2.82%
11.	EFDS	EFUNDS CORP	3.20%
12.	EK	EASTMAN KODAK CO	3.50%
13.	GAP	GREAT ATLANTIC & PAC TEA INC	3.88%
14.	GDW	GOLDEN WEST FINL CORP DEL	5.44%
15.	GYMB	GYMBOREE CORP	2.82%
16.	HAS	HASBRO INC	3.01%
17.	ITT	ITT INDS INC IND	2.82%
18.	LIZ	LIZ CLAIBORNE INC	2.91%

"Women Leaders" Portfolio (Firms with High Numbers of Female Executives) from FOLIOfn (continued)

#	SYMBOL	COMPANY	WEIGHT (% OF FOLIO)
19.	LU	LUCENT TECHNOLOGIES INC	3.20%
20.	MAPS	MAPINFO CORP	2.82%
21.	MLHR	MILLER HERMAN INC	2.91%
22.	MMM	3M COMPANY	2.91%
23.	NATR	NATURES SUNSHINE PRODUCTS INC	3.20%
24.	PBG	PEPSI BOTTLING GROUP INC	3.20%
25.	SCHL	SCHOLASTIC CORP	3.01%
26.	SY	SYBASE INC	2.82%
27.	TOY	TOYS R US INC	3.20%
28.	TR	TOOTSIE ROLL INDS INC	3.88%
29.	TUP	TUPPERWARE CORP	3.88%
30.	WLP	WELLPOINT HEALTH NETWORK NEW	3.69%

Source: FOLIOfn.

What Do Social Investors Look For?

Social investors share a broad common ground in their choice of portfolio screens. The most common screens are tobacco (96 percent of screened assets), gambling (86 percent), weapons (81 percent), alcohol (83 percent), and the environment (79 percent). Other screens include human rights (43 percent), labor (38 percent), birth control/abortion (23 percent), and animal welfare (15 percent). ❖

Source: The Social Investment Forum

What if You Can't Afford to Give?

Americans like giving to charity. But given the tough economic times we've experienced in the early 2000s, it's not so easy. So what can you do if you can't afford to open a socially

Build Your Own Mutual Fund

responsible personal portfolio or write a fat check to charity?

Until you can open your own SRI portfolio, do you want to try to come up with ways to give to charity without stretching your budget too much? The good news is that you can—if you're inventive.

Here's some ways to do just that:

• **Give your old car to charity**: If you have an old car lying around, in fair working order if not in actual use, consider giving it to charity. Groups like All-Donations.com and the Better Business Bureau currently administer highly specialized programs where citizens donate vehicles—including cars, trucks, trailers, and boats—to the organizations' 501-C nonprofit corporation charity clients. The organizations then give the vehicles to a charity of your choice, say, Meals on Wheels or the Salvation Army.

When you donate a vehicle to charity, you receive an IRS tax deduction for the fair market value, while avoiding all the headaches of selling a used car. That means no expensive want ads, no taking phone calls, no showing the car, no price haggling. Plus you'll also be assisting the charity of your choice.

• **Give less, but give often**: When people hit hard economic times, they stop giving to charity because they feel they can't afford to give. Some people even feel there's a stigma to giving less than $1,000 or even $100. That's just not so.

Thousands of charities would be more than happy to take donations as little as $5, $10, or $25. Sample charities may include your local school's cheerleading squad (so they can buy uniforms), Toys for Tots (so underprivileged kids can have Christmas presents), and many, many more. While you may not be giving as much as you like, you'll likely find yourself giving more often.

• **Donate time**: Business executives say that time is money. So if you can't give money, why not give time? Local community organizations, like hospices, homeless shelters, nursing homes, day care centers, even your local schools are always looking for helping hands. Besides pitching in and helping a worthy cause, you get a firsthand look at why you give to charity in the first place.

• **Donate old clothes:** Most communities these days have Salvation Army or Goodwill bins or other receptacles located on church parking lots or near shopping centers that accept clothing for homeless shelters and drug rehab centers to distribute to people down on their luck. Check with your local Salvation Army, Goodwill, or local parish or church for details on where you can donate clothing.

• **Donate food, canned goods, and other household items:** Hospices, nursing homes, schools, day care centers, homeless shelters, and other charitable organizations feel the economic pinch, too. If people are giving less, that just makes their jobs that much harder. So why not give food, toys, TVs, computers, and other household goods to such groups? They're all tax deductible and have the added benefit of bypassing administrative red tape that limits much of the cash-based charitable giving in the United States today.

• Lastly, just because you're giving less doesn't mean you shouldn't check out charities you're not familiar with. Never give to a charity you know nothing about. Ask for literature and read it. Ask questions. Honest charities encourage you to do so.

Case Study: *Making a Difference*

Michelle Stober was disgusted to find out the large-cap mutual fund she'd invested in included two or three companies that sold cigarettes. "I'm no saint, but I do like to make investment decisions with ethical and moral considerations in mind, as well as financial considerations," she says. "I don't have any illusions about closing a big tobacco company down—although that would be nice—I just want to use my money in a positive sense and with the hope of making a small difference."

Then a friend told Michelle about personal portfolios. "I couldn't believe I could build an investment portfolio with stocks that passed my ethical standards—I could never do that with a mutual fund." Working with a financial advisor, Michelle cashed out of the large-cap fund and used the proceeds to build her own fund that was mostly composed of companies that didn't sell cigarettes and were, in her view, good corporate citizens.

"I'd read that there was over $700 billion invested in socially responsible companies," says Michelle. "I wasn't surprised. I bet ten years from now there will be $700 billion more."

Michelle Stober Personal Portfolio

ALLOCATION PERCENTAGES

20% aggressive growth stocks
20% index mutual fund
20% international stocks
20% large-cap value stocks
20% cash

FOLIO FAVORITES

Duke Energy, Canon Inc., Nomura Holdings

Chapter Checklist

✓ Americans give over $200 billion annually to charity.

✓ Americans want to do more but are restricted in promoting social causes by their mutual fund investments, which give investors no control over the stocks that comprise their funds.

✓ Socially responsible investing traces its origins back to Jewish moneylenders 2,000 years ago.

✓ The idea behind SRI has really caught fire in the early 2000s, as more and more Americans want to tie their economic interests together with their social interests.

✓ Personal portfolios are an ideal vehicle for socially

responsible investing. Folio investors can choose the funds they want to include in their portfolios—and leave the ones they don't like out of the mix.

✓ When you choose socially responsible companies for your portfolio, use the same research elements you would in picking companies for a regular portfolio: good earnings, good management, good industry standing. Then ally the SRI elements that you care about: in other words, good environmental record, doesn't sell cigarettes, and so forth.

## Chapter 11

Fifty Ways to Build Your Mutual Fund

"To thine own self be true."
—WILLIAM SHAKESPEARE

I don't think you can squeeze every bit of information on personal portfolios in just one book. But this book is a great start.

Still, we're not through yet. Before you close the cover, I want to give you an opportunity to condense the key points you've read about in *Build Your Own Mutual Fund*. Plus, I want to give you some more specific tips to consider as you build your own fund. After all, you've already got the cake—now it's time for the icing.

What better way to do that than to list the fifty top things to know when creating your own mutual fund? These are some of my favorites—fifty in all:

1. **Have a plan**: During my senior year in college, when my campaign for my first professional job kicked off, my father only told me one thing: "Have a plan." Wise words indeed. Use the information in this book to develop a solid plan for building your own mutual fund and managing it effectively. Decide early on your level of risk, your asset allocation strategy, your investment style. Also decide if you want to use a financial advisor to help you build your personal portfolio.

2. **Set goals**: Any good marksman will tell you the key to hitting a target is having a target. Having something to aim at,

to work toward, gives you the framework for a successful personal portfolio plan.

3. **Be careful at first:** Ease your way into your personal portfolio. By that I mean don't throw $50,000 into your portfolio the very first week. Instead, invest a slice of your money the first week—say $5,000 of the $50,000—and get comfortable with the idea of being your own boss, portfolio-wise. Once you grow accustomed to your new sense of liberation and empowerment, you can shift into higher gear.

4. **Stick with your plan:** Things aren't always going to go the way you want them to. The only way you'll know when things begin to go awry is by monitoring your personal portfolio on a regular basis, say once or twice a week. My guess is you'll be so enthusiastic about running your own mutual fund you'll check in online once a day—or more. The trick is to track your plan and deftly steer it in a new direction if necessary.

5. **Include your spouse or partner in your personal portfolio:** Nobody likes surprises, so keep your loved one apprised of your personal portfolio plan. Talk about why you're doing it and the advantages of using personal portfolios. You don't want to dwell on it, but if something were to happen to you the last thing your spouse needs is to have an unfamiliar investment plan fall into his or her lap. Plus, by keeping your loved one informed, you'll have a good sounding board for your ideas and strategies.

6. **Have patience:** There's no formula I know of, outside of a winning Powerball ticket, to create financial security overnight. You're more apt to gain financial security over many years. So relax, monitor your progress, and enjoy the ride.

7. **Do your homework:** Read prospectuses, check company financial statements, watch CNBC, and keep this book handy. In short, do anything you can to bone up on the financial markets and the companies that trade on them.

8. **Reinvest your proceeds:** There's no rule that says you can't cash in and take some profits. Just don't make a habit of

it. Better to take the profits you make and plow them right back into some other winning stocks and bonds for your portfolio. That way, the miracle of compound interest is doing the heavy lifting—not you.

9. **Diversify your portfolio**: I've spent quite a bit of time on diversification in this book but with good reason. The lessons learned from the dot-com and Enron fiascos can't be understated. The best way to avoided being caught up in market volatility is to have your money spread around among different investments. When your investments are diversified, or spread across different asset classes or types of securities, they work together to help reduce risk. So go ahead and enjoy the benefits of slow and steady blue-chip stocks along with potentially higher-flying growth stocks. Mix in some U.S. Treasury notes with those international bonds. Spread the wealth and secure portfolio performance in the process.

10. **Invest in more than one asset class**: Try not to limit your investments to just one asset class. Even then, try to diversify within a particular asset class. For example, if you like the consumer goods sector, buy stocks in more than just one or two companies. By buying stock in a company that makes televisions and CD players and buying a company that makes toothpaste and soap, you're adding another level of diversity to your personal portfolio.

11. **Set price limits**: Professional Wall Street traders determine the price of a stock they're trying to buy or sell. If you can reasonably evaluate a dollar price where you feel okay getting in or getting out, it's easier to pull the trigger now that you have a price goal in mind.

12. **Don't gamble with money you can't afford to lose**: Betting junior's college fund on that hot telecom tip you heard about at the gym is a huge no-no. Keep your portfolio in perspective. Money you can't afford to lose does not belong in it.

13. **Don't be greedy**: If your stock research pans out and you have a stock that's risen by 50 percent or so since you bought it, take the money and run. It's not every day that you

own a stock that doubles in price. So cash out and try to find another one when that happens.

14. **Invest for the long haul:** Conversely, don't sell too quickly if a stock you like has some trouble gaining traction. Company stock prices will fluctuate, often downward, in the short term. But if you've done your research and the stock looks fundamentally sound, stay with it a while longer. So invest for the long term, but keep your current financial picture in mind.

15. **Don't be an impulse buyer:** It's tempting to deviate from your plan when you stumble across something you feel as if you simply have to own in your personal portfolio. Trust me and resist the urge. On Wall Street, impulse buyers usually regret their impulse buys. Only buy stocks when you've done the homework and had time to consider their addition to your personal portfolio.

16. **Look for value:** Undervalued stocks can really boost portfolio performance. If a company looks sound but its stock price is selling at a discount, chances are it's a worthy addition to your personal portfolio.

17. **Consider a financial advisor:** Having a professional shoulder to lean on once in a while can be a source of comfort to a do-it-yourself investor, especially one without significant investing experience. Hire a good advisor but continue to do your own homework and pick your own stocks. Run those picks by your advisor to see if they pass the smell test. Most personal portfolio companies offer some type of professional help.

18. **Stick to traditional stocks and bonds:** I started my career on Wall Street on an equity options trading floor and saw too many traders lose their shirts. And these were professionals. As you build your own mutual fund, you'll run across various pitches for options, futures, commodities, and other esoteric financial instruments. Stay away from them. They're complicated and not meant for the average investor. Even the professionals are burned by them on a regular basis. Stick with

stocks and bonds—they're easier to understand and have a relatively calming influence on your personal portfolio.

19. **Pick solid companies with a strong track record**: Emphasize stocks and bonds in companies that are among the leaders in their industries, regularly turn a profit, and have strong management teams. Focus on quality.

20. **Look for long-term growth with stocks**: In particular, look for growth stocks that have products and services that few others have, that have ample supplies of cash to weather tough economic times, and that do business globally (thus expanding the firm's chance of making money).

21. **Use your benchmarks**: If your portfolio leans toward large-cap stocks, make sure you're comparing its performance against a suitable index, like the Standard & Poor's 500. Likewise, if your personal portfolio is stocked with small companies, measure your performance against a small-company stock index, like the Russell 2000. A reliable yardstick is invaluable when evaluating the performance of your portfolio.

22. **Be the boss**: Never give a financial advisor the right to buy or sell without your prior approval. That way you won't have any surprises and you'll have control over what enters and leaves your personal portfolio. Remember that you're the one who has to live with the decisions made on your personal portfolio. Make sure you're making them—or at least signing off on the ones your advisor makes.

23. **Contribute to your personal portfolio on a regular basis**: Remember, a little investing, done on a regular basis, goes a long way. Investing monthly can add up over time:

Monthly Investment—$100

INVESTMENT PERIOD	TOTAL INVESTED	ACCOUNT VALUE
10 years	$12,000	$18,294
20 years	$24,000	$58,902
30 years	$36,000	$149,035

Note: Chart assumes $100 invested monthly for 10, 20, and 30 years and compounded at 8 percent.

24. **Check your ego/emotions at the door**: One of the biggest errors average investors make is investing with their emotions. When stocks rise, they buy; when they fall, they sell. That's exactly the opposite of what a successful investor should do. If you can't trust your emotions, then by all means run your portfolio selections by a professional advisor—or even trusted family member, friend, or spouse.

25. **Buy direct if you don't want to use a folio firm**: Many firms allow investors to buy stock directly from the company. These programs go by the names of Dividend Reinvestment Plans (DRIPs) or Direct Stock Purchases (DSPs). One drawback is that many of the most popular technology companies do not participate in these direct investment programs. In addition, many companies have added hefty fees to their direct stock purchase plans.

26. **Check out ShareBuilder**: Somewhere between folios and discount brokers is a Web site called Sharebuilder.com (discussed in Chapter 2). ShareBuilder enables you to buy more than 2,000 stocks for $4 a trade (or $12 a month for unlimited trading).

27. **Buy mutual funds if you want to**: There's no rule that says you can't invest in a personal portfolio and invest in a mutual fund, too. Ideally, you want to use one or the other. But once you build your own folio and you start enjoying the benefits of low-fee, low-tax, and high-customization personal portfolios, it's hard to turn back to mutual funds. That said, if you want to augment your stock-oriented personal portfolio with a bond fund or a money market fund, that's not a big deal. If you decide to go that route, consider a bond index fund. It's cheaper; it's tied to a reputable index that you can easily track; and it's usually safer than an actively managed fund.

28. **Find your investment style**: Are you a risk taker? Are you more conservative? Knowing your investment style is a critical component of your personal portfolio strategy. As a rule of thumb, your investment style is determined by your age, personality, financial experience, and financial circumstances.

29. **Allocate your assets**: You really can't go wrong by allocating your assets. Market experts say that roughly 92 percent of your investment returns depend on how your assets are spread out among various asset classes, while the remaining 2 percent of performance is due to your stock-picking abilities.

30. **Know your risk tolerance and time frame**: Knowing your risk tolerance will help you decide which personal portfolio strategy is right for you. For example, if you have a low risk tolerance, you may want to invest in a more conservative portfolio even though your time horizon indicates you could be more aggressive. Evaluating your time frame can be critical, particularly when building a personal portfolio based upon a projected retirement date.

31. **Time, not timing**: Trying to time the markets is akin to prospecting for fool's gold. Even if you were to guess correctly and earn greater returns on your investments, excessive trading can really foul up your portfolio and make it harder to build any momentum. Wall Street legend Warren Buffett has been quoted as saying that buy and hold is the best way to go. I'm not going to argue with Buffett on that score.

32. **Begin building your personal portfolio as soon as you can**: Consider the following hypothetical example. Karen began building her investment portfolio at age nineteen and earned a 10 percent annual growth rate on her investments. She contributed $2,000 per year between the ages of nineteen and twenty-six for a total of $16,000, before stopping her investment program at age twenty-seven. Even so, she'll have earned $1,035,148 by the time she reaches age sixty-five.

Now consider Kathy who waited until age twenty-seven to begin building her investment portfolio, earning the same 10 percent average annual return on her investment that Karen did. Overall, Kathy invests $2,000 per year starting at age twenty-seven and keeps on investing until age sixty-five, by which point she will have accumulated $883,185, which is approximately $120,000 less than Susan.

33. **Watch the analysts—closely**: Wall Street stock analysts have gotten in a kettle of hot water in recent years by trumpeting stocks in which their investment banking firms have a financial interest. So when you're researching a stock, look to see if an analyst's firm has underwritten the stock. You can find out by either reading the stock's prospectus or going online at the Securities and Exchange's EDGAR database. *(www.sec.gov/edgar.shtml).*

34. **Be sure to get the following information from your folio provider or discount broker**: Copies of completed account forms, agreements, and statements; and complete information about commissions, sales charges, penalties, maintenance or service charges, and transaction or redemption fees.

35. **Avoid trading scams**: Too many investors have been fleeced in nefarious investment scams. One of the most common on Wall Street is the "pump and dump" scam. In a nutshell, pump and dump means that fraudsters at small, thinly traded companies tout the company's stock on Internet Web sites in the form of gaudy press releases or via Internet chat rooms. Unwitting investors then eagerly buy the stock, creating high demand and pumping up the price. Soon, the scam artists sell their shares at the peak and stop touting the stock. After that the price plummets, and investors lose their money. Always consider the source when you hear about a hot stock. Also watch where the stock trades. Chances are a stock on the New York Stock Exchange is legit (they're very closely vetted before being listed) and NASDAQ stocks should be okay, too. But watch out for stocks that are listed as OTC (Over the Counter). Those stocks are more loosely regulated and more easily manipulated.

36. **Consider discount brokers**: If folios aren't your cup of tea, build your own mutual fund via the discount brokerage route. It will probably cost you more over the long run but most discount brokerage Web sites will help you set up your own portfolios and keep track of them. Here's a list of the fees charged by some of the more prominent discount brokerage firms:

Discount Brokers Fees—Minimum 500 Shares
(Through Dec. 31, 2002)

COMPANY	FEES
Financial Cafe	Unlimited Free Trades
American Express	Free (if have $25,000 in account)
Brown & Company	$5.00 (no help)
InvesTrade	$7.95
Suretrade	$7.95
Ameritrade	$8.00
Datek Online	$9.95
Waterhouse	$9.95
Regal	$14.95
Siebert	$14.95
Discover	$14.95
Fidelity Investments	$14.95
Quick & Reilly	$14.95
E-Trade	$19.95
DLJ Direct	$20.00
Charles Schwab	$29.95 (best resources)

37. **Consider an investing club**: Investment clubs—groups of investors who get together once a month or so to research stocks—are a great idea. It's a great way to meet other enthusiastic investors and turn up some interesting, thoroughly researched investment ideas.

38. **Bookmark these investment Web sites**: Two great (and free) investment sites are the Investment Company Institute *(www.ici.org)* and the Securities and Exchange Commission *(www.sec.org)*. Both are loaded with practical investment advice and great tutorials on investing, the economy, and the markets.

39. **When you sell a stock from your portfolio, replace it with another stock ranked first or second in its industry**: Once again, it's a quality issue.

40. **Know why stocks move**: Historically, stocks move in one direction or another for two reasons:

The first is the perception by investors of the firm's financial fortunes. If it appears that the company will make money, investors will likely buy the company's stock at a premium, or higher price. That will cause the stock's price to rise. But if it looks like the company is going to lose money, investors will likely avoid buying the stock (or sell it if they own it). That will cause the stock's price to decline.

The second reason a stock's price may fluctuate is investors' perception of the overall stock market—or at least the industry or sector the company resides in. If, for example, the company makes automobile parts, then the stocks may only do as well as the auto industry. Or, if the stock is in the large-cap sector, its fortunes may be tied, fairly or unfairly, to the fortunes of all large-cap stocks.

41. **Watch out for "fast-moving markets"**: Market traders are like sharks in that they often hunt in packs and engage in feeding frenzies from time to time. Remember the red-hot Internet Public Offering (IPO) stocks of the go-go 1990s? People couldn't wait to buy them even as the stock price's rose quickly. If you didn't get in early you lost out. If you do find yourself chasing a hot stock, you may find that trading in the stock is slow because the pack smells blood and everybody wants in. Trade executions slow to a crawl and prices change so fast that the price you wanted to buy the stock at can be much lower than the price you wind up buying it at. To mitigate the impact of a fast market, know what you're buying, and set price limits on buy and sell orders so you don't get burned.

42. **Have a good PC and Internet line**: Always a good idea, but especially in fast-moving markets. Without a fast, reliable computer with a speedy Internet connection, you might find technological "logjams" can slow or prevent trade orders from reaching the trading floor. If worse comes to worst, and your computer crashes or the server at your trading firm crashes, make sure the firm offers other options for trade execution, like phone and fax numbers. Just don't expect a quick execution.

43. **Wait for your trade confirmation**: A common mistake among do-it-yourself investors is not waiting for their trade confirmations before re-entering the same order. Being impatient is understandable in the financial markets, but re-entering a trade before getting a confirmation is foolhardy. Often there is a delay in the pipeline that causes news of your trade's execution to be slow in coming. But the order was executed. Often investors who don't wait for confirmation of a trade will re-enter the order and wind up owning twice as much stock as they wanted to—at twice the price.

44. **Cancel a trade? Okay, but make sure it's really canceled**: If you cancel a trade order, make sure the cancellation clears before placing another trade. Why? Because if a trade isn't really canceled, it could still show up in your personal portfolio and you'll be held liable for any money owed. Check with your trading firm to see what kind of cancellation policy they have.

45. **Act fast if you have a trading problem**: Don't dither if you have a bad trade or other order error. The longer you wait, the worse your chance of gaining satisfaction in any dispute. Contact your trading firm right away if you think there's been a trading problem. Speak to a manager if you have to, but be sure to get an answer. If that doesn't get you any relief, contact your trading firm's legal advisor, preferably by e-mail or direct mail (so you have written documentation of the problem). If you're still not getting a satisfactory response, contact the National Association of Securities Dealers, your state securities administrator, or the Office of Investor Education and Assistance at the SEC and send copies of the letters you've sent already to the firm. Reach the SEC at *www.sec.gov/investor/pubs/onlinetips.htm*.

46. **Take your portfolio firm for a test drive**: To gauge a folio firm or discount broker's customer service capabilities, give them a call in the middle of the day to see how fast you can get a response. Ideally, do this before you pick a trading firm.

47. **Ask around**: Ask your trading firm for a list of qualified references. Or check out a company's reputation on one of the many investment chat rooms on the Word Wide Web. A good place to start is the Motley Fool at *www.fool.com.*

48. **With discount brokers, vet them thoroughly**: Take a peek at the firm's charges per transaction, and test their reliability and speed in executing orders before signing on to build your personal portfolio. One trick: E-mail the discount broker a question to see how long it takes to get an answer.

49. **Check out the following Web sites when researching a company's financial status**:

Standard & Poor's *(www.standardandpoors.com)*
Moody's Investors Services *(www.moodys.com)*
Weiss Ratings *(www.weissratings.com)*

50. **Lastly, have fun**: You're your own boss now and the personal mutual fund you create will have your personal stamp on it. So enjoy all the benefits and all the power that personal portfolios provide. Heck, take some of the money you've saved in fees and taxes and buy you and your loved one a nice bottle of champagne. Open it and toast the new financial you. As you sip the bubbly, consider how far you've come in taking control of your financial life. After all, nobody has as much invested in your financial future as you do.

## Chapter 12

Will Folios Surpass Mutual Funds?

"Success is a science.
If you have the conditions, you'll get the results."
—OSCAR WILDE

The writer and humorist Bill Bryson once wrote that there are three things you can't do in life: you can't beat the phone company, you can't make a waiter see you unless he's ready to see you, and you can't go home again.

Now we can add a fourth item to that list: you can't go back to mutual funds once you've learned how to build one yourself. Even the mutual fund industry acknowledges that. Otherwise, why would they be in such a hurry to roll out their own folio programs?

The fund industry knows a tsunami is coming. In a do-it-yourself world where you can custom-build your own new car online, plan your own trip to Australia, and create your own Web site for that new home-based business you're starting, they know what I've spent the last 300 pages telling you—why shouldn't you be able to build your mutual fund?

The rising tide of personal portfolios may be bad news for the mutual fund industry, but it's great news for investors. They're already heading into personal portfolios in large numbers.

A recent report by Forrester Research, Inc. of Cambridge, Massachusetts, called "The End of Mutual Fund Dominance," predicts more than $1 trillion will flow out of funds over the next ten years. Currently, Forrester pegs total fund assets in 2002 at $6 trillion. The report also says that the bulk of the cash outflows will go into separately managed folio accounts, which will garner 20 percent of all investable assets by 2010.

Boston-based Cerulli Associates is just as bullish on the separate account industry. According to its October 2002 "Market Update: The Managed Accounts and Wrap Industry," during the mid to late 1990s, consultant wrap assets advanced between 20 and 30 percent per year, much like the mutual fund industry and the U.S. equity markets. "Going forward, we expect consultant wrap assets to increase about 30 percent to 40 percent per year in the next three to five years," says Cerulli. And an October 2000 cover story in *Red Herring* entitled "The Death of Mutual Funds" raised eyebrows all over Wall Street.

Such dramatic denunciations of mutual funds and subsequent praise for do-it-yourself investment accounts are no surprise to financial industry observers.

Says Steve Wallman, president and founder of FOLIO*fn*, the rise of the do-it-yourself portfolio is just beginning. "Mutual fund companies that previously viewed the fund vehicle as their only delivery mechanism for their investment management expertise have started to discover efficient 'folios' and separately managed accounts to offer investment management to those who have outgrown one-size-fits-all mutual funds," says Wallman. "And this is just in time, as funds are growing hardly at all, and many are experiencing net outflows."

Until now, Wallman says, there have been two preferred means of delivering advice and management. "One is through mutual funds. Funds cater well to the general investment population but are not personalized, tailored or tax-efficient forms of investing, although they are easily distributed and ubiquitous.

"The second means is through a brokerage, with advisers and full-service representatives delivering advice and recommendations for active, personalized, tax-efficient management. In general, however, it has been difficult to deliver well-diversified separately managed portfolios with the exception of expensive programs geared toward the affluent investor."

Wallman's view is that the Internet revolution has primed the pump for a third way to invest—by building your own personal portfolios. "Technology now permits offerings that easily combine the advantages of both individual stocks and mutual funds. Direct securities ownership provides an investor with control and flexibility as well as tax efficiency, whereas mutual funds provide an investor with much needed diversification and professional portfolio management. The advantages of the two would be a perfect investment."

That's the beauty of personal portfolios. They provide all of those advantages at a cost that permits professional money management and advice to be offered to a wide range of investors. And it's just the beginning, he says. "The first wave of the Internet was met with too much expectation and failed to live up to all of the hype. But in reality, the Internet is changing the world."

It's a change that we're already seeing. According to Charlie Bevis, editor-in-chief of research studies at Financial Research Corp. and author of a new series of reports on the future of the fund industry, the industry financial services will grow to encompass more than just mutual funds. His data show that the ratio of mutual fund assets to personal portfolio assets has dropped from 15 to 1 at year-end 1996 to 10 to 1 at the end of 2001.

He's not alone. Gavin Quill, Senior Vice President of *FRC Monitor*, a magazine that covers the financial services industry, says that personal portfolios will grow and that the growth of mutual funds will abate in the coming years. "Over the next three to five years, the growth in separate accounts—primarily the generic or modified separate accounts serving the upper middle class—will come largely at the expense of mutual funds. What I mean by modified is that firms will adapt the technology they've developed for large private accounts serving the very wealthy and apply it cost-efficiently to smaller accounts; that is, for those who are migrating up the wealth scale. We already see minimum investment requirements coming down.

"The growth in exchange-traded funds and stock baskets or folios will come at the expense of brokerages," he adds. "Our research shows that the increased market share for separate investment accounts is coming from individual stock purchasers."

In other words—people just like you and me. So, in the future—probably a lot sooner than conventional wisdom seems to think—more and more investors from both the mutual fund and brokerage worlds will convert some or all of their fund assets into personal portfolios.

Yes, it may take some time for the superior benefits that do-it-yourself fund building provides—flexibility, lower fees, easier tax management, and complete control and customization—to hit home to investors. But in an investment era plagued by scandals and poor performance, more investors will turn to personal portfolios to give them more control over their financial futures and to fight back against the entrenched powers on Wall Street that say there is only one way to invest. That's old thinking.

I started this book with a quote from one of the mutual fund industry's living legends, John C. Bogle, founder and former chairman of the Vanguard Group. Let's end it with another quote from Mr. Bogle, a guy who's been around Wall Street for decades and knows what he's talking about. "Sooner or later, intelligent investors will exhibit the kind of investment behavior that serves their own best interests."

With personal portfolios, it's happening sooner than Wall Street thinks.

Glossary

asset: Assets include any of an individual's possessions that have economic value. The sum of his or her assets is considered to be the individual's net worth. Assets include stocks, bonds, cash, real estate, jewelry, investments, and other properties. For personal portfolio investors, establishing your current assets is a critical first step in building your own mutual fund.

asset allocation: Asset allocation refers to the specific distribution of funds among a number of different asset classes within an investment portfolio; it is diversification put into practice. Funds may be distributed among a number of different asset classes, such as stocks, bonds, and cash funds, each of which has unique types of expected risk and return. Within each asset class are several variations of the asset, meaning that there are levels of risk within each asset class. Asset allocation involves determining what percentage of funds will be invested in each asset. Determining how to allocate funds depends on the individual investor. The investor's goals, time frame, and risk tolerance will all affect how an investor wishes to allocate funds based on the investor's desired return and acceptable risk. Personal portfolio investors can create their own asset allocation strategies or use one of the many formulas advocated by financial experts. These formulas are easy to find on the Internet. Simply go to *www.google.com* and type in "asset allocation strategies."

bear: Someone who believes or speculates that a particular security, or the securities in a market, will decline in value is referred to as a bear. Investors are "bearish" when they view stocks as being in sustained decline.

bear market: A bear market is a market in which a group of securities falls in price or loses value over a period of time. A prolonged bear market may result in a decrease of 20 percent or more in market prices. A bear market in stocks may be due to investors' expectations of economic trends; in bonds, a bear market results from rising interest rates.

bid price: The price a prospective buyer is ready to pay. This term is used by traders who maintain firm bid and offer prices in a given security by standing ready to buy or sell security units at publicly quoted prices.

blue chip: Blue chip refers to companies that have become well established and reliable over time, and have demonstrated sound management and quality products and services. Such companies have shown an ability to function in both good and bad economic times and have usually paid dividends to investors even during lean years. Most blue chips are large-cap, *Fortune* 500–type stocks like IBM or General Electric.

bond: A bond is essentially a loan made by an investor to a division of the government, a government agency, or a corporation. The bond is a promissory note to repay the loan in full at the end of a fixed time period. The date on which the principal must be repaid is called the *maturity date,* or *maturity.* In addition, the issuer of the bond—that is, the agency or corporation receiving the loan and issuing the promissory note—agrees to make regular payments of interest at a rate initially stated on the bond. Interest from bonds is taxable, based on the type of bond. Corporate bonds are fully taxable; municipal bonds issued by state or local government agencies are free from federal income tax and usually free from taxes of the issuing jurisdiction; and Treasury bonds are subject to federal taxes but not state and local taxes. Bonds are rated according to many factors, including cost, degree of risk, and rate of income.

bottom-up analysis: The search for outstanding performance of individual stocks before considering the impact of economic trends. Such companies may be identified from research reports, stock screens, or personal knowledge of the products and services.

bull: Someone who believes that a particular security, or the securities in a market, will increase in value is known as a bull. Investors are "bullish" when they view stocks as being on the upswing.

bull market: A bull market is a long period of rising prices of securities, usually by 20 percent or more. Bull markets generally involve heavy trading and are marked by a general upward trend in the market, independent of daily fluctuations. Example: from 1982 to 2000 American investors enjoyed two lengthy bull markets, one lasting from 1982 through 1990 and the other lasting from 1992 through 2000.

capital gain distributions: Payments to a mutual fund's shareholders of profits earned from selling securities in a fund's portfolio. Capital gain distributions are usually paid once a year.

capital gains: A capital gain is appreciation in the value of an asset—that is, when the selling price is greater than the original price at which the security was bought. The tax rate on capital gain depends on how long the security was held. Studies show that personal portfolios are much easier, tax-wise, when it comes to declaring capital gains, than are mutual funds.

certificate of deposit: A certificate of deposit (CD) is a note issued by a bank for a savings deposit that the individual agrees to leave invested in the bank for a certain term. At the end of this term, on the maturity date, the principal may either be repaid to the individual or rolled over into another CD. The bank pays interest to the individual, and interest rates between banks are competitive. Monies deposited into a certificate of deposit are insured by the bank; thus, they are a low-risk investment and a good way of maintaining a principal. Maturities may be as short as a few weeks or as long as several years. Most banks set heavy penalties for premature withdrawal of monies from a certificate of deposit.

commission: Commission is a fee charged by a stockbroker or, in some cases, the financial advisor may be working with an investor on a personal portfolio, who makes transactions of buying or selling securities for another individual. This fee is generally a percentage based on either the number of stocks bought or sold or the value of the stocks bought or sold.

credit risk: Credit risk refers primarily to the risk involved with debt investments, such as bonds. Credit risk is essentially the risk that the principal will not be repaid by the issuer. If the issuer fails to repay the principal, the issuer is said to default.

default: To default is to fail to repay the principal or make timely payments on a bond or other debt investment security issued. Also, a default is a breach of or a failure to fulfill the terms of a note or contract.

discount broker: Brokerage firms that offer cut-rate fees for buying stocks, usually online over the Internet (although discount brokers also offer phone and fax trade order options). Some of the most prominent include Charles Schwab, Quick & Reilly, and Ameritrade.

diversification: Diversification is the process of optimizing an investment portfolio by allocating funds to a number of different assets. Diversification minimizes risks while maximizing returns by spreading out risk across a number of investments. Different types of assets—such as stocks, bonds, and cash funds—carry different types of risk. For an optimal portfolio, it is important to diversify among assets with dissimilar risk levels. Investing in a number of assets allows for unexpected negative performances to balance out with or be superseded by positive performances.

dividend: A dividend is a payment made by a company to its shareholders; that is, a portion of the profits of the company. The amount to be paid is determined by the board of directors, and dividends may be paid even during a time when the company is not performing profitably. Mutual funds also pay dividends. These monies are paid from the income earned on the investments of the mutual fund. Dividends are paid on a schedule, such as quarterly, semiannually, or annually. Dividends may be paid directly to the investor or reinvested into more shares of the company's stock. Even if dividends are reinvested, the individual is responsible for paying taxes on the dividends. Unfortunately, dividends are not guaranteed and may vary each time they are paid.

dividend yield: The current or estimated annual dividend divided by the market price per share of a security.

Dow Jones Industrial Average: The Dow Jones Industrial Average is an index to which the performance of individual stocks can be compared; it is a means of measuring the change in stock prices. This index is a composite of thirty blue-chip companies ranging from AT&T and Hewlett-Packard to Kodak and Johnson & Johnson. These thirty companies represent not just the United States; rather, they are involved with commerce on a global scale. The DJIA is computed by adding the prices of these thirty stocks and dividing by an adjusted number that takes into account stock splits and other divisions that would interfere with the average. Stocks represented on the Dow Jones Industrial Average make up between 15 percent and 20 percent of the market.

earnings growth: A pattern of increasing rate of growth in earnings per share from one period to another, which usually causes a stock's price to rise.

equity: Equity is the total ownership or partial ownership an individual possesses minus any debts that are owed. Equity is the amount of interest shareholders hold in a company as a part of their rights of partial ownership. Equity is considered synonymous with ownership, a share of ownership, or the rights of ownership.

financial advisor: A fully accredited financial planning professional who helps people manage their money, prepare for retirement, manage their taxes, and prepare an estate planning strategy (among other financial services). Financial advisors are a good idea for do-it-yourself investors who want a good sounding board as they build their own mutual funds.

folio: Popularized by companies like FOLIO*fn* and E*Trade, folios are an ideal mechanism for building your own mutual fund. Essentially folios are "baskets" of stocks that do-it-yourself investors pick on their own. Some folio companies also provide "ready to go" folios of selected stocks. Folio programs can cost as little as $29.95 per month to use.

fundamental analysis: An analysis of the balance sheet and income statements of a company in order to forecast its future stock price movements. Fundamental analysts consider past records of assets, earnings, sales, products, management, and markets in predicting future trends in these indicators of a company's success or failure. By appraising a company's prospects, these analysts assess whether a particular stock or group of stocks is undervalued or overvalued at its current market price.

going public: A company that has previously been privately owned is said to be "going public" the first time the company's stock is offered for public sale.

growth investing: An investment style that emphasizes companies with strong earnings growth. Growth investing is generally considered more aggressive than "value" investing.

hedge: Hedging is a strategy of reducing risk by offsetting investments with investments of opposite risks. Risks must be negatively correlated in order to hedge each other—for example, an investment with high inflation risk and low immediate returns with investments with low inflation risk and high immediate returns. Long hedges protect against a short-term position, and short hedges protect against a long-term position. Hedging is not the same as diversification; it aims to protect against risk by counterbalancing a specific area of risk.

inflation: Inflation is a general increase in prices coinciding with a fall in the real value of money, as measured by the Consumer Price Index.

inflation risk: Inflation risk is the risk that rising prices of goods and services over time—or, generally the cost of living—will decrease the value of the return on investments. Inflation risk is also known as purchasing-power risk because it refers to increased prices of goods and services and a decreased value of cash.

interest rate: Rate of interest charged for the use of money, usually expressed at an annual rate.

junk bond: Junk bonds are bonds that are considered high yield but also have a high credit risk. They are generally low-rated bonds and are usually bought on speculation. Investors hope for the yield rather than the default. An investor with high risk tolerance may choose to invest in junk bonds.

liquidity: Liquidity refers to the ease with which investments can be converted to cash at their present market value. Additionally, liquidity is a condition of an investment that shows how greatly the investment price is affected by trading. An investment that is highly liquid is composed of enough units (such as shares) that many transactions can take place without greatly affecting the market price. High liquidity is associated with a high number of buyers and sellers trading investments at a high volume.

market capitalization: The market price of a company's shares multiplied by the number of shares outstanding. Large-capitalization companies generally have over $5 billion in market capitalization; medium-cap companies between $1.5 billion and $5 billion; and small-cap companies less than $1.5 billion. These capitalization figures may vary depending upon the index being used and/or the guidelines used by the portfolio manager.

market risk: Market risk is the risk that investments will lose money based on the daily fluctuations of the market. Bond market risk results from fluctuations in interest. Stock prices, on the other hand, are influenced by factors ranging from company performance to economic factors to political news and events of national importance. Time is a stabilizing element in the stock market, as returns tend to outweigh risks over long periods of time. Market risk cannot be systematically diversified away.

market value: Market value is the value of an investment if it were to be resold, or the current price of a security being sold on the market.

modern portfolio theory: Aims to minimize the risks of investing while maximizing returns through the diversification of a portfolio. Diversification is the process of allocating funds among a number of different asset classes. Modern portfolio theory looks at three main factors in determining appropriate investments for an investor's portfolio: (1) the investor's goals and objectives for investing, (2) the time frame of the investment, and (3) the investor's risk tolerance, or how comfortable the investor is with taking certain risks. Optimizing a portfolio according to modern portfolio theory involves matching the statistics of expected risk and return for a number of different assets with the individual's terms of investment.

mutual fund: Mutual funds are investment companies whose job is to handle their investors' money by reinvesting it into stocks, bonds, or a combination of both. Because mutual funds are divided into shares and can be bought much like stocks, they have high liquidity. Mutual funds are convenient, particularly for small investors, because they diversify an individual's monies among a number of investments. Investors share in the profits of a mutual fund, and mutual fund shares can be sold back to the company on any business day at the net asset value price. Mutual funds may or may not have a load, or fee; however, funds with a load will provide advice from a specialist, which may help the investor in choosing a mutual fund. Many do-it-yourself investors have grown weary of excessive tax liability, high fees, and restricted control of mutual funds. That's why so many have switched to personal portfolios.

NASDAQ (National Association of Securities Dealers Automated Quotation): The National Association of Securities Dealers Automated Quotation is a global automated computer system that provides up-to-the-minute information on approximately

5,500 over-the-counter stocks. Whereas on the New York Stock Exchange (NYSE) securities are bought and sold on the trading floor, securities on the NASDAQ are traded via computer.

NASD (National Association of Securities Dealers): The National Association of Securities Dealers is an organization of broker-dealers who trade over-the-counter securities. The NASD is self-regulated. The largest self-regulated securities organization, this organization operates and regulates both the NASDAQ and over-the-counter markets, ensuring that securities are traded fairly and ethically.

NYSE (New York Stock Exchange): Established in 1792, the New York Stock Exchange is the largest securities exchange in the United States. Securities are traded by brokers and dealers for customers on the trading floor at 11 Wall Street in New York City. The exchange is headed by a board of directors that includes a chairperson and twenty representatives who represent both the public and the members of the exchange. This board approves applicants as new NYSE dealers, sets policies for the exchange, oversees the exchange, regulates members' activities, and lists securities.

personal portfolio: The same idea as a folio, personal portfolios are baskets of stocks that do-it-yourself investors select on their own or with the help of a financial advisor. Some investors choose to bypass the folio route and use a discount broker to build their own personal portfolio.

price-earnings ratio: The price-earnings ratio is a measure of how much buyers are willing to pay for shares in a company, based on that company's earnings. The price-earnings ratio is calculated by dividing the current price of a share in a company by the most recent year's earnings per share of the company. This ratio is a useful way of comparing the value of stocks and helps to indicate expectations for the company's growth in earnings. It is important, however, to compare the P/E ratios of companies in similar industries. The price-earnings ratio is sometimes also called the "multiple."

price-to-book ratio: Current market price of a stock divided by its book value, or net asset value.

productivity: This measurement is defined as output per hour of work; increases in it can finance wage hikes.

quotation: A quotation, or quote, refers to the current price of a security, be it either the highest bid price for that security or the lowest ask price.

real rate of return: The real rate of return refers to the annual return on an investment after being adjusted for inflation and taxes.

reinvestment: Reinvestment is the use of capital gains, including interest, dividends, or profit, to buy more of the same investment. For example, the dividends received from stock holdings may be reinvested by buying more shares of the same stock.

return on equity: The amount, expressed as a percentage, earned on a company's common stock investment for a given period. It is calculated by dividing net income for the period after preferred stock dividends but before common stock dividends by the common stock equity (net worth) average for the accounting period. This tells common shareholders how effectively their money is being employed.

Securities and Exchange Commission (SEC): The Securities and Exchange Commission is a federal government agency comprised of five commissioners appointed by the President and approved by the Senate. The SEC was established to protect individual investors from fraud and malpractice in the marketplace. The commission oversees and regulates the activities of registered investment advisors, stock and bond markets, broker-dealers, and mutual funds.

security: A security is any investment purchased with the expectation of making a profit. Securities include total or partial ownership of an asset, rights to ownership of an asset, and certificates of debt from an institution. Examples of securities include stocks, bonds, certificates of deposit, and options.

socially responsible investing: A mechanism for investors to invest in companies that pass their ethical standards. Personal portfolios are good ways to invest in socially responsible companies because they give investors a way to pick and choose the companies that comprise their portfolios. With mutual funds, money managers do all the stock picking and investors have no say in the matter.

S&P (Standard & Poor's) 500 Index: The S&P 500 Index is a market index of 500 of the top-performing U.S. corporations. This index, a broader measure of the domestic market than the Dow Jones Industrial Average, indicates broad market changes. The S&P 500 Index includes 400 industrial firms, 20 transportation firms, 40 utilities, and 40 financial firms.

split: A split occurs when a company's board of directors and shareholders agree to increase the number of shares outstanding. The shareholders' equity does not change; instead, the number of shares increases while the value of each share decreases proportionally. For example, in a 2-for-1 split, a shareholder with 100 shares prior to the split would now own 200 shares. The price of the shares, however, would be cut in half; shares that cost $40 before the split would be worth $20 after the split.

technical analysis: The research into the demand and supply for securities, options, mutual funds, and commodities based on trading volume and price studies. Technical analysis uses charts or computer programs to identify and project price trends in a market, security, mutual fund, or futures contract.

ticker: The ticker displays information on a movable tape or, in modern times, as a scrolling electronic display on a screen. The symbols and numbers shown on the ticker indicate the security being traded, the latest sale price of the security, and the volume of the most recent transaction.

top-down approach: The method in which an investor first looks at trends in the general economy, selects attractive industries, and then picks companies that should benefit from those trends.

total return: The change in value of an investment in a fund over a specific time period expressed as a percentage. Total returns assume all earnings are reinvested in additional shares of a fund.

underwriter: An underwriter is an individual who distributes securities as an intermediary between the issuer and the buyer of the securities. For example, an underwriter may be the agent selling insurance policies or the person distributing shares of a mutual fund to broker-dealers or investors. Generally, the underwriter agrees to purchase the remaining units of the security, such as remaining shares of stocks or bonds, from the issuer if the public does not buy all specified units. An underwriter may also be a company that backs the issue of a contract by agreeing to accept responsibility for fulfilling the contract in return for a premium.

value investing: A relatively conservative investment approach that focuses on companies that may be temporarily out of favor or whose earnings or assets are not fully reflected in their stock prices. Value stocks will tend to have a lower price-earnings ratio than growth stocks.

volatility: Volatility is an indicator of expected risk. It demonstrates the degree to which the market price of an asset, rate, or index fluctuates from the average. Volatility is calculated by finding the standard deviation from the mean, or average, return.

yield: Yield is the return, or profit, on an investment. Yield refers to the interest gained on a bond or the rate of return on an investment, such as dividends paid on a mutual fund. Yield does not include capital gains.

Index

A

All or None (AON) orders, 154
American Association of Fundraising
Counsel (AAFRC), 195–96
American Stock Exchange, 156
ask (term), 155
asset allocation
explanation of, 112–14, 232
importance of, 114, 222
mistakes in, 184
in personal portfolios, 117–19,
124–26
and risk, 120–26
strategy, 115–19
See also diversification
asset classes, 22, 92, 106–8, 112–14
assets, 34–37, 232
Atlantic Richfield, 200

B

bank statements, 54–56
Baruch, Bernard, 164
Baxter International, 201
bear/bear markets, 167–69, 232
Beebower, Gilbert L., 114
behavioral finance, 142–47
benchmarks, 158–59
Bevis, Charlie, 230
bid/bid price, 155, 232–33
blue-chip stocks, 84, 233
Bogle, John C., 1, 231
bonds, 67–69, 80, 93–94, 98, 107,
108, 110, 112–14, 116–22, 169, 233
Boston's Financial Research Corp., 2
bottom-up analysis, 233
Brinson, Gary P., 114
Brokerage America, 17–18
brokers/broker-dealers, 78, 223–24,
226–27, 229–30, 235
bubbles, 76–77, 142–43
budgets, 39–48
See also spending records
Buffett, Warren, 77, 82, 222
bull/bull market, 233, 234
business inventories, 99
BuyandHold.com, 17

C

cancellations, 226
capital gain distribution, 234
capital gains and losses, 171–76, 234
capitalization, 59
certificate of deposit, 234

Certified Consumer Credit
Counselors (CCCCs), 186
Certified Financial Planners (CFPs),
185–86
Certified Public Accountants (CPAs),
186
Cerulli Associates, 10, 229
charitable donations, 195–96, 211–13
See also socially responsible
investing
Charles Schwab, 5, 184
Chartered Financial
Consultants/Chartered Life
Underwriters (ChFCs/CLUs), 186
Chicago Board of Trade Web site, 86
close (term), 155, 157
commissions, 78, 234
company effect, 74
confirmations, 226
conservation, 59
consolidation, 59
consumer confidence, 100–101
Consumer Price Index (CPI), 100
CorporateRegister.com, 207
cost basis, 173–74
credit cards, 40, 46, 54–56
credit reports, 43
credit risk, 94, 235
Crosswalk.com, 207
CSRwire.com, 207
currency risk, 94
cyclical markets, 77

D

Daily Close (Close), 155, 157
day orders, 153–54
debts, 34–39, 41–42, 134
default (term), 235
Direct Marketing Association, 56–57
Direct Stock Purchases (DSPs), 221
diversification, 7–8, 27, 38, 86–88,
94, 103–10, 124, 139–40, 168, 235
See also asset allocation
Dividend Per Share (Div), 157
dividend reinvestment plans (DRIPs),
171, 221
dividends, 72–73, 109, 132, 134, 171,
235
dividend yield, 157, 236, 243
Dollar Cost Averaging (DCA), 119–20
The Dollar Stretcher, 46
Domini 400 SocialSM Index (DSI),
208–10

About the Author

Brian O'Connell is a Bucks County, Pennsylvania, writer with ten books to his credit. A former Wall Street bond trader, O'Connell is married with three children. E-mail him at *brian.oco@ verizon.net* or visit his Web site at *www.brianoc.com*.